# Ages & Stages
# Learning Activities

# Ages & Stages
# Learning Activities

by

Elizabeth Twombly, M.S.

and

Ginger Fink, M.A.

·P A U L·H·
BROOKES
PUBLISHING Cº ®

Baltimore • London • Sydney

**Paul H. Brookes Publishing Co.**
Post Office Box 10624
Baltimore, Maryland 21285-0624

www.brookespublishing.com

Manufactured in the United States of America by
Versa Press, Inc., East Peoria, Illinois.

Third printing, August 2007.

Visit **www.agesandstages.com** and see the order form at the end of this book to learn more about the complete **ASQ** and **ASQ:SE** systems.

**Library of Congress Cataloging-in-Publication Data**

Twombly, Elizabeth.
    Ages & stages learning activities / by Elizabeth Twombly and Ginger Fink.
       p.    cm.
    "These activities have been designed to coordinate with Ages & stages questionnaires (ASQ) : a parent-completed, child-monitoring system, second edition"—Introd.
    Includes bibliographical references.
    ISBN-13:978-1-55766-770-0
    ISBN-10:1-55766-770-5
    1. Early childhood education—Activity programs.   2. Child development.   3. Infants—Development.
  I. Title: Ages and stages learning activities.   II. Fink, Ginger.   III. Bricker, Dinane D. Ages & stages questionnaires.   IV. Title.

LB1139.35.A37T96   2004
155.4'028'7—dc22
                                                            2004043557

British Library Cataloguing in Publication data are available from the British Library.

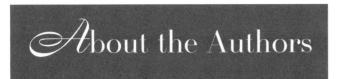
# About the Authors

**Elizabeth Twombly, M.S.,** lives in Eugene, Oregon, and is Senior Research Assistant of the Early Intervention Program at the University of Oregon, Eugene. Prior to working in the field of early intervention, Elizabeth spent many years working with young children in environmental education, child care, and preschool programs on the east and west coasts. Elizabeth has been involved in the *Ages & Stages Questionnaires® (ASQ)* project since the early 1990s and was involved in the initial development and research for the *Ages & Stages Questionnaires®: Social-Emotional (ASQ:SE).* She trains across the nation on the implementation of these screening tools in a variety of health and educational programs that work with families with very young children. Elizabeth is coordinating projects in the Early Intervention Program that relate to screening systems and infant mental health.

**Ginger Fink, M.A.,** has worked in the field of early childhood education for more than 30 years. She has worked in many capacities as a teacher, director, curriculum developer, and teacher educator. She is a private consultant in the area of parent–child programs and teacher education strategies.

She worked as curriculum developer from 1987 to 1996 for the Kamehameha Schools, Honolulu, Hawai'i, toward development of a statewide series of community-based parent–child programs. She also worked extensively with Head Start programs as teacher and program director intermittently between 1966 and 1975, and as disabilities specialist between 1997 and 2000 for the Region X training and technical assistance network. She also served as the training coordinator for the *Ages & Stages* developmental screening system for the University of Oregon, Eugene. In addition to private consultation, she teaches early childhood courses at Clackamas Community College, Oregon City, Oregon.

# Acknowledgments

We wish to acknowledge the continued encouragement that Jane Squires gave us to complete this project. Thank you for all of your support, gentle reminders, and ultimately—a hard deadline! In addition, we wish to acknowledge and thank the Hawai'i Infant Child Monitoring Questionnaire task force members who made significant contributions to this effort including Winnifred Ching, Robin Einzig, Barbara Essman, Clare Kohatsu, and Patsy Murakami. We also thank friends in the administration of and the preschool division of the Kamehameha Schools and Ruth Ota, R.N., B.S.N., M.P.H., Chief, Public Health Nursing Branch, Hawai'i State Department of Health, who continues to work tirelessly for the children of Hawai'i.

# Introduction

Welcome to the *Ages & Stages Learning Activities*. These activities have been designed to coordinate with *Ages & Stages Questionnaires® (ASQ): A Parent-Completed, Child-Monitoring System, Second Edition* (Bricker & Squires, 1999). These simple activities were designed to provide parents, home visitors, teachers, and others with quick, inexpensive ideas for learning games and interactions that enhance the growth and development of infants and young children. These activities are written in simple language and use materials that most families have on hand at home.

In addition to supporting areas of development, it is the authors' hope that these activities strengthen the parent–child relationship. To this end, the activities are designed to be playful, fun, and affectionate. The authors hope that these activities will bring laughter and joy to the family. Although the *Ages & Stages Learning Activities* are designed for use with the ASQ system, they are appropriate to use independent of a screening or monitoring program.

## THE ASQ AND AGES & STAGES LEARNING ACTIVITIES

The ASQ is a series of parent-completed questionnaires that screen and monitor a child's development between 4 months and 5 years of age. The results of a questionnaire determine if a child is currently developing at an age-appropriate level or if he or she should receive a more in-depth assessment from a local early intervention/early childhood special education agency to determine the need for specialized services. The ASQ screens development in the areas of communication, gross motor, fine motor, problem solving, and personal-social skills.

Because a parent or caregiver, not a professional, completes the ASQ, the ASQ provides an inexpensive method for screening and monitoring a child's development. Screening with the ASQ elicits three potential results:

- *Well above the ASQ cutoffs:* The child appears to be developing typically at this point in time.
- *Below the ASQ cutoffs:* The child falls on or below a statistically derived cutoff and should be referred to a professional to determine if he or she is eligible for specialized services.
- *Close to the ASQ cutoffs:* The child falls close to a cutoff; the score is questionable and the child appears to need some additional support in one or more developmental areas. At this time, however, the child is not showing a delay that is significant enough to warrant a referral.

The *Ages & Stages Learning Activities* are designed to be used to follow up with children who receive a result of *well above the ASQ cutoffs* or *close to the ASQ cutoffs* when screened using the ASQ. If a child scores below the cutoffs and is referred and determined not eligible for specialized services, the learning activities also can be used. However, these activities are not intended to be a comprehensive intervention that meets the needs of a child with an identified developmental delay. As mentioned previously, these children should be receiving in-depth individualized instruction from an early intervention or early childhood special education provider. If appropriate, the activities could be used to support an intervention program.

The *Ages & Stages Learning Activities* are organized to coordinate with the ASQ and are grouped according to 1) age of the child and 2) area of development. While the ASQ system includes 19 questionnaires, *Ages & Stages Learning Activities* contains 12 sets. Table 1 provides guidelines as to which age range of the Learning Activities should be provided following screening with the ASQ.

## AGES & STAGES LEARNING ACTIVITIES SHEETS

There are five activity sheets in each set of the Learning Activities: communication, gross motor, fine motor, problem solving, and personal-social. Although it is recognized that every activity a child engages in can provide opportunities to practice and enhance multiple skills, these activities focus on one specific area at a time so that caregivers concentrate their attention on each specific area. In addition, the pronouns *he* and *she* alternate throughout the series of activities, but the activities are intended to be appropriate for either boys or girls.

Following a screening, program staff members have the option of providing a full set of Ages & Stages Learning Activities to a caregiver or selecting specific areas

**Table 1.** ASQ and *Ages & Stages Learning Activities* age-range guidelines

| After screening with the ASQ questionnaire for | Provide the following set of *Ages & Stages Learning Activities* for |
| --- | --- |
| | 1–4 months |
| 4 months | 4–8 months |
| 6 months | 4–8 months |
| 8 months | 8–12 months |
| 10 months | 8–12 months |
| 12 months | 12–16 months |
| 14 months | 12–16 months |
| 16 months | 16–20 months |
| 18 months | 16–20 months |
| 20 months | 20–24 months |
| 22 months | 20–24 months |
| 24 months | 24–30 months |
| 27 months | 24–30 months |
| 30 months | 30–36 months |
| 33 months | 30–36 months |
| 36 months | 36–42 months |
| 42 months | 42–48 months |
| 48 months | 48–54 months |
| 54 months | 54–60 months |
| 60 months | |

depending on screening results. For example, a child at 12 months may receive a result of *well above the ASQ cutoffs* in the areas of communication, gross motor, problem solving, and personal-social but a result of *close to the ASQ cutoff* in the fine motor area. In this case, staff can choose to provide caregivers with a full set of 12- to 16-month activities or with only the 12- to 16-month fine motor activities.

Each activity sheet includes a brief description of what might be typical in terms of development at that specific age span. Because development is different for each child, a child's skills may or may not be reflected in this description. It is important for caregivers to be responsive to the unique developmental needs and strengths of each child.

After the brief developmental description, a series of between five and eight age-appropriate activities are provided. The activities provide opportunities to develop a variety of skills in each developmental area and to practice skills that are targeted on the ASQ screening; however, these activities should not be considered all inclusive. Children learn from adults in hundreds of ways, and these are just a few. Some may be new; many others are time tested and familiar. We hope that parents will add to these activities from their own experiences. Home visitors and other helping professionals are invited to add to these suggestions or to modify activities to meet a specific child's or family's needs.

In each set of activities, the authors have included games or activities that support language and literacy development. We hope that some of the foundations of literacy will be encouraged in every child's home, such as experimenting with rhythm and rhymes; gesturing; speaking; listening; reading books, magazines, newspapers, and signs on the street and in stores; experimenting with writing tools by scribbling, drawing, creating grocery lists, and writing letters and cards to loved ones; and so forth. The love and enjoyment of reading as well as success in later formal school situations can be rooted in these early childhood years.

Adaptations may be necessary to respectfully support families whose first language is not English or who come from diverse cultural backgrounds. Although these activities are written in English, the authors hope that home visitors or parents will feel free to adapt them to their home language and to add games from their tradition or experience. All cultures have special favorite baby games, rhymes, and songs. When a baby hears these loving sounds, his or her knowledge of who he or she is will be strengthened. In some cases, a learning activity may not be something a family might choose to teach. For example, some families may not wish to engage their children with mirrors. Respect for the family's values must guide the interactions and choices.

Activities are written at a fourth- through fifth-grade reading level. Although this reading level may meet the needs of many families, other families may need additional support. Activities may need to be demonstrated, illustrated, or shared verbally with families. For example, a home visitor can introduce a new activity to a family each week, bringing specific toys or helping family members gather materials in their home environment. Of course, it is important to consider safety guidelines for children at each developmental level. Although some of the activities include safety precautions, an adult should supervise all activities that involve young children. Use the activities with flexibility.

## REFERENCE

Bricker, D., & Squires, J. (with Potter, L., Nickel, R., & Farrell, J.). (1999). *Ages & Stages Questionnaires®: A Parent-Completed, Child-Monitoring System* (2nd ed.). Baltimore: Paul H. Brookes Publishing Co.

# Communication

## Activities to Help Your Baby Grow and Learn

Your wonderful new person communicates with her whole body. Her gaze at you tells you that you are the most important person in the world. She communicates with body movements, noises, and her own special cry when she needs something. Your baby's favorite music is your gentle voice. Even though she enjoys the sounds of a busy household, some quiet time is important so baby can hear family voices.

**Song and Rhyme**  Introduce your baby to the chant, rhyme, and rhythm of your favorite songs and nursery rhymes. Change the words of a familiar tune. Add baby's name now and then ("Twinkle, twinkle, little Andy. How I love my little Andy").

**Sing and Talk as You Take Care**  As you bathe, feed, exercise, or change your baby, sing any song. Make up your own songs. Let your baby watch your face while you talk and sing. Encourage other family members to do this. Baby knows how important she is.

**Funny Baby**  During quiet, happy times encourage your baby to smile. Make funny (not scary) faces that baby likes. When baby smiles, be sure to make that face again. Tell baby how funny he is!

**Picture Books**  With baby cuddled on your lap, hold a book with simple, clear, colorful pictures so that both of you can see. Talk softly about what you see as you point to the pictures. Baby will learn that reading time is very special.

**Special Talking Time**  When your baby is awake, cuddle her and hold her so she can see your face. Talk for a little while. Look at her face as she looks at yours. Encourage her to make different sounds, coos, and squeals. Have a conversation.

**Words for Baby's Cry**  As you comfort baby when he cries, talk about why he is crying. Try to figure out what's wrong, and tell him about it as you take care of his needs.

**Noticing Sounds**  When sounds happen around the house, help baby notice by talking about them ("I hear the telephone ringing," "I hear your brother calling").

**Telephone Time**  When you are on the phone, hold your baby close and look at her. Baby will enjoy watching and listening to you. She'll think your conversation is just for her!

Ages&Stages

1–4 months

# Gross Motor
## Activities to Help Your Baby Grow and Learn

Baby is gaining strength right from the beginning. He practices lifting and controlling his head. He moves his arms and legs. Soon he will be able to roll to his side from his back. He likes being held so that his feet gently touch a surface. He likes to be held in a sitting position so that he can strengthen his back and tummy muscles and see what's going on.

**Position Changes**
When baby is awake, place baby in a different position, on her stomach or side. This will allow baby to move her arms and legs in different ways or directions. Always watch baby when she's on her stomach.

**Kicking Practice**
Place baby on his back on a firm surface. As you talk quietly to baby, encourage him to move his legs. Hold a foot in each hand and gently move them back and forth.

**Heads Up**
Put baby on her stomach. Dangle a bright toy in front of her, or make faces and sounds to encourage your baby to lift her head.

**Bath Time**
One special way to bathe baby is in the tub with you. Enjoy gently massaging his legs, arms, tummy, and back. Allow baby to kick and splash as you hold him safely and talk and sing a little bathtub song.

**Balancing Act (about 3–4 months)**
Stand baby on your knees and gently hold her in a standing position. Let her support as much of her own weight as she can to help her strengthen her legs and gain balance.

**Roll Over**
Encourage baby to roll from his stomach to his back by holding a bright toy in front of him and slowly moving it over to the side. You may help him roll over until he can do it himself.

**Pretty Pull-Ups (about 3–4 months)**
With baby on your lap, pull baby up slowly by her arms. Then, gently lower her in an up-and-down game. Talk to her as she moves up and down. This will help to strengthen stomach muscles and let baby see the world and your smiling face from a different point of view.

Ages&Stages

1–4 months

# Fine Motor
## Activities to Help Your Baby Grow and Learn

Your baby is gaining control of her gaze and can focus on a nearby object for a few seconds. Soon she'll be able to follow you with her eyes while you move around. Her fist will grasp your finger and hold on tightly. She will show excitement by waving her arms. It is a wonderful time of beginning to notice what's going on in the world!

**Finger Kiss**
When feeding baby, encourage him to touch your lips (if he doesn't do this spontaneously). Kiss his fingertips. Baby will learn the soft, wet sensation of your lips and soon will learn to aim his fingers toward your lips.

**Gotcha (about 3–4 months)**
While your baby is lying on a rug or sitting in her infant seat, offer a toy or something to grasp just beyond her reach. When she reaches for it, make sure she gets it. She'll probably taste it, too.

**Finger Grip**
Let your baby grab your finger and grip it tightly. Gently tug a little just to let your baby know you're there. "My, you are so strong!"

**Finger and Toe Rub**
Rub your baby's fingers and toes one at a time. A little baby lotion makes this especially nice. Your baby will enjoy the sensation. It will increase his body awareness.

**Ribbon Flutter**
Hang a long, brightly colored ribbon or scarf loosely around your neck. When you lean over to change baby or pick her up, let her reach out and touch the ribbon. Sit and talk about what she is doing.

**Tug-O-War**
Let baby grasp a dishcloth or the corner of a washcloth. Gently tug the other end. Tell him how strong he is. Let go, and let him win!

Ages & Stages

1–4 months

# Problem Solving

## Activities to Help Your Baby Grow and Learn

Your baby already responds to sounds and voices. He's beginning to look for the source of the noise. He also looks at his surroundings and will show an active interest in a person or toy. He likes to study things like his own hands and his favorite face—yours!

| | |
|---|---|
| **Tracking Fun** | Let baby follow a rattle, a shiny spoon, or your face with his eyes. Hold your face or an object 10–12 inches from baby's face and slowly move from left to right. Talk softly as you play. Baby will enjoy being part of the action. |
| **Light Touch** | Stroke your baby gently with a feather, a cotton ball, or the edge of a cloth. Your baby will enjoy the sensation as she learns to isolate different body parts. Talk to baby softly. Describe what she is feeling. |
| **Cotton Ball Sniff** | To help your baby develop his sense of smell, dip cotton balls in different fragrances such as mint or vanilla extract. Gently waft these near baby so he can experience the scent. "Mmm, it smells so good." |
| **Making Faces** | With baby on her back, lean over her and make surprised or happy faces. Encourage her to reach for your nose or lips or mouth. Have a little laugh together. |
| **Colorful Socks** | Put a brightly colored sock on your baby's foot. This will encourage her to look at her feet, then pull at them and catch a foot. This game will help baby discover parts of her own body. |
| **Silver Spoons** | Lie your baby on his back, and dangle a shiny spoon above him so he can reach and bat it. A shiny spoon also makes a nice hanging crib toy to entertain baby as long as it is safely tied out of reach. |
| **Reaching Practice (about 3–4 months)** | With your baby in your lap or the lap of another special person, hold up a safe, interesting toy on a string for him to reach for. Let baby be successful by slowly moving the toy to his fingers. |

Ages&Stages

1–4 months

# Personal-Social
## Activities to Help Your Baby Grow and Learn

Baby will look into your eyes to tell you "I'm yours." She loves and needs a lot of holding and physical contact. When she needs you, she will fuss or cry. Your response and gentle voice will comfort her. When she is taking in information, she will be calmer. This is often after eating, resting, or having a diaper changed. At about 7 weeks old, she will respond with a beautiful smile!

**Love and Trust Building**
Respond right away when baby cries. It's her way of telling you something important. Carry, hug, smile, sing, and talk to baby often. It's your way of saying, "I love you and I'll take care of you."

**Communicating Through Touch**
After his bath, baby may be ready for a massage. Use baby oil and gently massage his arms, hands, legs, feet, back, tummy, and bottom. Continue only as long as your baby is quiet and content. Talk or sing a little song. You can make it up—baby won't mind.

**Funny Face Play**
Make an "oh" face; stick out your tongue or pucker your lips when baby seems to be studying your face. Hold that expression and see if your baby will imitate it. Smile if baby copies you!

**Looking in the Mirror**
Hold your baby up in front of a mirror. She may enjoy smiling and making noises at herself. As baby looks in the mirror she is learning about your gentle touch and about the "other" baby she sees.

**Peekaboo**
Play Peekaboo with your baby. Place your hands over your eyes then over baby's eyes. Release your hands and say, "Boo." Place a blanket over your head and come out saying, "Boo." Your baby will enjoy many variations of this game for a long time to come.

**Happy Hands**
As baby's fist begins to relax, place a small toy in his hand. He won't be very good at letting go just yet. Let him grasp your finger while you nurse. Later, guide his hands to hold his bottle. Smile and tell him how strong he is!

Ages&Stages

1–4 months

Your baby has learned to use his voice: He squeals and is beginning to babble to you and to others. He knows his name and may use his voice to let you know he is happy. He can shout for your attention and is about to make sounds such as "mama" or "dada." He is also learning to respond to "bye-bye."

| | |
|---|---|
| **Baby Rubdown** | After bath time, enjoy some quiet time talking with your baby as you gently rub him down with lotion or oil. Tell him about your day—ask about his. |
| **What's That?** | When your baby notices a sound, help her locate the source. Ask your baby, "What's that? Daddy's car?" "Did you hear a dog?" |
| **Touch that Sound (about 5 months)** | As your baby begins to experiment with his voice, you will probably hear /b/, /m/, and /d/ and "ah," "ee," and "oo" sounds. Imitate the sounds baby makes. While you make the sound, let your baby put his fingers on your lips to feel the vibrations. |
| **Trust Building with Words** | When you move away from your baby to do other things, keep in touch with your baby through your words. Tell her what you are doing as she follows with her eyes. "I'm over here. I'm picking up the clothes. I'll be right back." Now and then step out of sight, but continue to talk until you return. "Did you miss me?" |
| **Reading Time** | Your baby will enjoy looking at pictures in magazines or books. Choose things such as a telephone, dog, car, or spoon. Sit with your baby on your lap and read about the pictures. Tell a little story. "See the phone? It's for you." |
| **Sing a Song** | When you are bathing, diapering, or changing your baby's clothes, sing a song such as "This is the way we wash our toes, wash our toes, wash our toes. This is the way we wash our toes, so early in the morning." |
| **Hide-and-Seek** | Move just out of sight and call baby's name. Wait a few seconds, and then reappear. "Here I am!" Now find another place and hide again. |

Ages&Stages

4–8 months

# Gross Motor
## Activities to Help Your Baby Grow and Learn

Your baby gets stronger every minute. She now holds her head up and looks all around at everything that's going on. She is learning to sit by herself, even though at first she uses her hands for support. She loves bearing her weight on her legs and will soon pull to stand.

**Floor Time** — Spread out a quilt on the floor or outside under a tree. Put your baby on the blanket on her tummy with a few of her favorite toys and encourage her to stretch, scoot, roll, squirm, or wiggle her way to the toys. Be sure to give some time for baby to be on her back, too.

**Sitting Pretty** — Help your baby sit alone. Sit behind him and give him some gentle support. He can hold a toy or a book. Whisper in his ear that he is a wonderful baby! As he learns to sit by himself, you can give him less help.

**Bouncy Baby** — Hold on to your baby's hands and help her stand up. Have fun bouncing up and down while she's standing on the floor, the sofa, or your lap. Sing a little bouncing chant: "Bouncy, bouncy, bouncy, stop. Isn't that fun?"

**Stand-Up Play** — At about 7 months your baby may enjoy standing up while holding on to tables and chairs and reaching for different objects. Remove breakable items from low tables or shelves, and line up some of his favorite toys to reach for.

**Little Explorer** — Now that baby can crawl, she'll want to explore the whole house! Make sure the areas where she can explore are safe and clean. "What's under the table? What's behind the chair?" What good exercise!

**Obstacle Course (about 6–7 months)** — Once your baby has started to crawl, you can make a simple obstacle course of pillows and blankets for your baby to crawl across and around.

**A Shiny Pot Lid (7–8 months)** — As your baby gets better at sitting alone, give your baby a pan or pot lid to play with. He can see himself in the pan as he bangs it, pats it, and rolls it.

4–8 months

# Fine Motor
## Activities to Help Your Baby Grow and Learn

Your baby's grasp has relaxed now, and he likes to reach and grab nearby objects. He can hold and bang objects and even hold something in each hand! He may watch you scribble with interest. He's learning how to use his fingers and is getting better at it every day.

**Rattles and Toys**  Give your baby plenty of opportunities to try out different rattles and toys. Things that feel different or toys that make sounds will be very interesting to your baby. Some of the best toys aren't toys at all, such as spoons.

**Picky, Picky (6 months or older)**  When your baby starts eating solid food, he will enjoy trying to pick up small bits with his thumb and forefinger. Don't worry about the mess. This fun activity strengthens eyes and fingers.

**Mello Jell-O**  Make small Jell-O cubes. Your baby will love to catch the Jell-O as it squirms around on her plate.

**Drop and Dump**  As soon as your baby can sit alone, he can sit on the floor and play some dropping games. Use a plastic container and a small ball, block, or toy. Let your baby drop the ball into the container. You may need to help him at first. Now dump it out. He will want to try it again and again!

**Finger-Paint**  Put a dab of soft, smooth food (e.g., yogurt; soft, mashed carrots) on a plate or cookie sheet and let your baby "paint" with her fingers. It's all right if she eats the "paint."

**Noodle Pull**  Give baby a little serving of cool, cooked noodles. Let baby pull apart a few strands. This is a fun way to practice using fingers and to snack at the same time. (Always stay attentive while baby eats.)

**Cheerios Spill**  Put some Cheerios in a plastic bottle. See if your baby can figure out how to tip over the bottle to feed himself the Cheerios.

**Tub Time**  Make bath time fun. This is a good time to practice holding, pouring, and squeezing. Add plastic cups, pitchers, sponges, and scoops to baby's bath. What wet, bubbly fun!

Ages&Stages

4–8 months

# Problem Solving
## Activities to Help Your Baby Grow and Learn

Your busy learner is interested in making things work! She will find a toy that's partly hidden and will reach with all her might for something that's just out of reach. She knows when a voice is friendly or angry and much prefers friendly sounds. She also loves Peekaboo!

**Where Did it Go?** Move your face or a favorite toy behind a cover while your baby is watching. Ask, "Where is Mommy?" Drop the cover and say, "Here I am!" Cover baby's doll or bear. Ask, "Where is the bear?" Move the cloth and say, "There he is!"

**Bath-Time Boats** Put a fleet of plastic butter containers in your baby's bath. She will delight in learning about sinking, floating, dumping, and pouring.

**Reactions** Provide baby with toys that react such as squeak toys, pull toys, and pop-up toys. Let baby discover ways to make things happen! Share baby's surprise. "Look what happened!"

**Hide a Squeak Toy** Hide a toy or some item that makes noise, such as a bell or set of measuring spoons, under a blanket while your baby watches. Reach under the blanket and make the sound. Let him try to find it. Now hide the toy to the side, then behind your baby. Let him look around.

**Music Maker** Give baby a spoon or a block for each hand. Show her how to bang them on a tabletop or highchair tray while you sing a song. Sing and tap loudly, then sing and tap very softly. Hooray for the band!

**Hide a Baby** This is a fun version of Peekaboo. While folding laundry or doing the dishes, cover baby with a sheet, towel, or dishcloth. Say, "Where's the baby?" Wait a second and pull down the cloth. "Surprise! There's the baby!"

**Safe Sandbox** In a small container or tray, let baby touch some cornmeal or flour. As you do this, talk about how it feels and show him how to sift it through his fingers. "Ooh, that's so soft."

Ages&Stages

4–8 months

# Personal-Social
## Activities to Help Your Baby Grow and Learn

Your baby knows you very well now and will lift his arms to come to you. He may begin to fret when strangers approach. He likes to play with his image in the mirror and is really quite sociable as long as he feels safe and secure.

**A Cup for Baby**  Allow your baby to hold a plastic cup. Put a little water in it, and see what baby will do. She will probably enjoy trying to drink out of a cup. Let her experiment.

**Body Awareness**  Your baby is discovering different body parts and probably has become very interested in his feet and hands. Encourage him by playing games such as This Little Piggy and other games with fingers and toes. Talk about his body when he touches his feet. Say, "You found your feet!"

**Self-Feeding**  Encourage your baby to pick up and eat safe foods such as crackers or Cheerios. You may also give baby her own spoon to hold while you feed her with another spoon. Try taking turns—you pretend to eat a little and then offer a bite to your baby. Baby will understand that feeding herself is the way to go.

**Whisper Power**  Rock, walk, or dance and whisper sweet words in your baby's ear. Whispering to your baby helps him to calm down and provides another way to talk in a quiet and loving voice.

**A Social Hour**  Invite another parent and his or her baby over to play with your baby. As the babies look at, reach for, and explore each other, they will make important discoveries about real people. Stay close by to keep each baby safe as they do their exploring.

**Wave Bye-Bye**  Wave bye-bye when you leave the room for a moment or two. As you wave, tell your baby where you are going. "I am going into your bedroom to get your blanket. I'll be right back. Bye-bye."

**Faces in the Mirror**  While looking in the mirror with your baby, talk about body parts such as the eyes, nose, and ears. Touch your nose and say, "Daddy's nose!" Touch baby's nose and say, "Baby's nose." "Daddy's eyes, baby's eyes." Play this game as long as baby seems interested.

Ages&Stages

4–8 months

# Communication

## Activities to Help Your Baby Grow and Learn

Your baby now has many different sounds and a lot to say. She likes to play with sounds such as "ba ba ba" and is learning that some sounds mean special people, such as "dada." She understands some words and directions now and will soon say the names of familiar people or things.

| | |
|---|---|
| **Following Directions** | Help your baby to learn to listen and follow simple directions. Try simple directions such as "Show me Grandma," "Wash your tummy," or "Hold the diaper." When baby responds or follows the direction, be sure to let him know you notice. "Oh, there's Grandma" or "Thank you for holding the diaper." |
| **Grocery Time Is Learning Time** | When you go to the grocery store and baby is with you, talk to her about what she is seeing. Let her hold a box or put items into the grocery cart. Point out signs in the store and read them to your baby. "That sign says apples. Let's get some nice red apples." |
| **The Telephone Game** | Talk to your baby on his play phone or an old cellular phone. When there are two phones, you can both talk and your baby will have fun carrying on a conversation just like the big people. |
| **Sleep Waltz** | At naptime or bedtime in the evening, hold your baby close and dance together to some quiet music. Your baby has probably spent a lot of time exploring during the day. Now she needs some cuddling. This communicates to baby a feeling of closeness and intimacy. |
| **Quiet Times** | When baby is awake and alert, turn off the radio and TV so that he only hears your voice. This helps baby hear the sounds of words more clearly. Hum and sing just for baby's pleasure. Ask baby, "Can you hear a bird?" "Can you hear the clock?" |
| **Baby Babble Game** | When your baby makes a sound such as "ba," repeat the sound back: "ba ba ba." Your baby will enjoy playing with sounds and making conversation. |
| **Applause, Applause** | When baby does something new or fun, give baby a hand. Clap and say, "Yea!" Baby will love the attention and will probably clap, too! |
| **Reading Adventures** | Read to your baby every day. Cuddle up, get close, and make this a special time together. Point to pictures in books or ask her to find something. "Where's the kitty?" |

Ages&Stages

8–12 months

# Gross Motor
## Activities to Help Your Baby Grow and Learn

This is a very active period for your baby. He's now pulling up on furniture, crawling and creeping into places he couldn't reach before, and getting ready to walk. In fact, he will probably walk holding on to your hand and attempt a few steps without your help. Baby is on the move.

**Money in the Bank**   Save round metal ends from frozen juice containers or lids from jelly jars to use as "money." Now that your baby can sit alone, let her put these round things into a clear container. Then shake the container and make a great noise. Dump them out and put the "money" in the bank again.

**Kick, Kick**   When you are changing your baby's diaper or getting him ready for bed, play this game. As your baby kicks his legs, sing in rhythm to the kicking. When your baby stops kicking, stop singing. When he starts again, start singing. This will develop into a fun game of stop and go. Your baby not only exercises his muscles, but he gets to be the boss.

**Reaching for Fun**   If your baby is pulling himself to a standing position, put some of her favorite toys on a low table and let her stretch way out to reach them. This will give her practice with reaching and balancing. She will also be learning about ideas such as near and far.

**Rain, Rain in the Tub**   Get a small empty plastic container, put some holes in it, and let your baby fill it with water during bath time. Help him hold it up and discover "rain" for himself while you supervise.

**Walking Practice**   Once your baby has started to walk, she will want to practice a lot. Show her how to hold on to a lightweight chair or stool and push it around the room. Sturdy cardboard boxes also make great push toys, as does a stroller. Let your baby push a stroller when you go for walks.

**Tunneling**   While folding laundry, throw a sheet over a table or the backs of two chairs. Let your little explorer crawl into the "tunnel." When he's out of sight, call him. Then, greet him with surprise when he finds you.

Ages&Stages

8–12 months

# Fine Motor
## Activities to Help Your Baby Grow and Learn

Your busy baby is beginning to pick up tiny bits of food with her thumb and fore-finger. She can take things out of a container, such as spoons out of a plastic bowl, and can bang two toys together. If you give her a crayon and paper, she may even attempt to imitate your writing with a scribble.

**Feely Game**  Make a feely game out of a cardboard box by including things to feel, hold, and bang. Good items might include an empty plastic baby bottle, a square of velvet fabric, and a sponge. Let baby reach into the box and grab something. Talk about what he is holding. This exercise for little muscles also helps baby explore different textures.

**Hand Clapping**  Help your baby bring her hands together and clap. Clap her hands and then hide them under a blanket. She will like to watch her hands go away and come back.

**Catcher's Up**  Use a small, soft ball—or make a ball out of socks rolled together—and play catch with your baby. He won't be able to really catch the ball yet, but he will enjoy trying to throw it and chase after it.

**Tearing**  If baby loves to tear paper, get a big basket or box and put some old magazines and wrapping paper inside. Let your baby tear what she wants. If she is more interested in putting wads of paper in her mouth, put the box away and try again in a few weeks.

**Sticks and Stones**  Take a walk outside. Encourage your baby to gather stones in a pail or small paper bag. Pick up twigs and leaves. Talk about the color or the size. "Look—this big leaf is nice!" (Remember to watch out for things that might go into your baby's mouth.)

**Goodies in a Jar**  Put Cheerios or small pieces of cereal in a screw-top or snap-top plastic jar or snap-top butter container. Put the lid on loosely. Let baby take the lid off. You may have to show your baby how to take the lid off and get the cereal. Soon he will do it by himself.

**Bedtime Book Time**  A great way to get ready for bed is to snuggle up and read books with your baby. Let her pick a few books and help turn the pages. Talk about the pictures, and enjoy your special time.

Ages&Stages

8–12 months

As baby learns how things work, he is busy taking them apart. He can take pieces out of a puzzle or rings off of a stack. He is learning how to find hidden objects under a blanket. He enjoys looking at pictures in a book and enjoys your naming the pictures. He's been so busy exploring that he probably now knows the word "no."

**Rhythm Play**    Using small blocks or spoons, try drumming on the table or clapping toys together to make sounds. Sing along and dance a little. Enjoy the music.

**Scarf Pull**    Tie several colorful scarves together. Insert one end into a cardboard tube. Let your baby pull the scarves through the tube. Now, can your baby stuff the scarves back into the tube?

**Hide-and-Seek**    Hide a ticking clock or a small radio under a pillow or blanket. Let your baby listen to find the sound. "Do you hear it?" "Where is it?"

**A Third Toy**    Give your baby a third toy when she has a toy in each hand. See if she can figure out a way to take the third toy and hold on to all three. If this is too difficult for your baby right now, try it again in a few weeks.

**In and Out**    Put a piece of cereal inside a clear plastic container or baby bottle without a lid. As your baby works to get the cereal out, he will learn more about inside and outside. Another way to show baby the ideas of inside and outside is to get a big box that your baby can crawl in and out of.

**Little Laughs**    By about 11 months, your baby will begin to develop a sense of humor. Do something funny such as trying to drink out of her baby bottle or pretending to put on her shoe when getting ready to go out. She will probably burst out laughing.

**Magic Cups**    Place a cup and a small toy on a tray for baby. Hide the toy under the cup and ask, "Where is the toy?" If he doesn't find it, lift the cup and show your baby where it is. Say, "You found it!" Do this several times. Soon he will lift the cup and find the toy all by himself. Later, add another cup. See if baby can remember which cup hides the toy.

Ages & Stages

8–12 months

 **Personal-Social**
Activities to Help Your Baby Grow and Learn

Your baby may fear strangers and prefer only you. She loves to explore her environment and needs your watchful eye to keep her safe. She shows her likes and dislikes and shows affection to you and even a favorite toy. She can help you dress her but likes to do things by herself when she can.

| | |
|---|---|
| **Bath Time** | When your baby is taking a bath, give her the washcloth. Encourage her to wash by herself. After the bath, let your baby help get dressed by pushing her arm through her nightshirt. Be patient; these self-help skills take a lot of time and practice. |
| **Follow Me** | Your baby probably is learning to enjoy imitation. Encourage this by showing your baby how to play Follow the Leader with you. Use simple movements, such as tapping on the table or putting a hat on your head. Talk about what you are doing. Say, "Your turn," and see if your baby will follow along. Let your baby have a turn at being the leader. |
| **Party Time** | Your baby may enjoy watching older children play. This is especially fun when there are older brothers or sisters. If there are other babies his own age in the neighborhood, he will enjoy playing alongside them. At first they will enjoy watching each other. Eventually, they will learn to play together. |
| **Little Helper** | Give your baby a damp sponge, and let her wipe the table, chairs, floor, walls, and doors. This is an activity she may enjoy doing while you are getting dinner ready or washing dishes. Tell baby, "Thank you for helping Mommy." |
| **Snack Time** | Your baby will enjoy feeding himself during snack time. Give him a few choices of simple foods such as crackers, pieces of fruit, or cheese. He'll even enjoy trying to drink out of a big boy cup with a little help. |
| **Mirror, Mirror** | When you have a moment at home or while running errands, stop and encourage your baby to look at her face in a mirror. Make silly faces. Tell her what a big girl she is getting to be. |
| **Roly-Poly Game** | While sitting on the floor, roll a small ball to baby, and then ask him to roll it back. Now, do it again. Then, do it just a little faster! This could be a fun game to play with an older sister or brother. |

 Ages&Stages

**8–12 months**

# Communication

## Activities to Help Your Baby Grow and Learn

Your baby's babbling is beginning to sound more like talking. He says "mama" and really means it and is beginning to learn the names of things. He may say "no" if he is not happy. Because he's so busy learning to walk, his language use may slow down a bit. He combines a word with a point or gesture and you know very well what he means.

| | |
|---|---|
| **Hide the Noises** | Show your baby three things that make noise, such as a squeak toy, a set of measuring spoons, and a rattle. Let baby play with them for a while. Then hide the items under a box or cloth and make a noise with one. Take the cloth off and ask baby, "Which one made the noise?" See if she can guess. |
| **Quiet Time** | On weekends or at some time that's not busy, spend time with baby in a quiet place with no radio and no TV, perhaps outside. Talk to your baby about what you're doing or about what baby is doing. Let your baby hear your voice and see your face making words. Talk calmly and tell baby how special he is. When your baby talks, encourage him. Have a conversation. |
| **Rhythm Clapping** | While listening to music, show baby how to move and clap in rhythm. Your baby will enjoy moving to the beat. Play different types of music, such as rock and roll, country, and classical music. |
| **Listening on the Telephone** | When Daddy or Grandma calls, ask them to spend a few minutes talking to baby. Baby probably won't talk back to them yet but will be delighted to hear someone's voice coming through the telephone. |
| **Big Talk** | While you do housework or get a meal together, talk to your baby about what you are doing. Encourage your little one to use two words together to make baby sentences, such as "Help me," or "More juice." This big language step will grow into a lot of talk. |
| **Little Reader** | Read to your baby every day. Cuddle up and make this a special time. Point to pictures and name things for her. Sometimes ask her to find something: "Where's the cat?" She may need a little help from you at first. |
| **Big Helper** | Your baby can be a big helper. Give him simple directions: "Can you get me a napkin?" "Give me your shirt." He may need you to point or help a little. Say, "What a big help. Thanks!" |

Ages & Stages

12–16 months

# Gross Motor
## Activities to Help Your Baby Grow and Learn

By now your busy baby can move around the house quickly. She may be standing by herself, walking while holding on to furniture, or walking well. She will try to climb up steps, and your watchful eye is very important. Baby loves to push and pull things and is getting stronger every day.

**Let's Go for a Walk**     Your baby will love going for walks and seeing new things. Talk to her about what you are seeing. In an open area, let baby push her own stroller. She will enjoy the feeling of power as she moves something big all by herself. Be sure to watch that she keeps the stroller where it's safe.

**Row the Boat**     Let your child experience rocking on a rocking horse or in a chair. Sit him on your lap and use your body to rock back and forth. Play with him sitting opposite of you on the floor. Hold hands and gently pull and push him to and from you. Sing a little song, such as Row, Row, Row Your Boat, while you rock back and forth.

**Tunnel Time**     Drape a sheet or bedspread over a table or two chairs so that it becomes a tunnel. Encourage baby to crawl through. "Come on through." "There you go." "You made it!" Siblings will have fun playing this game, too.

**Roll a Ball**     Your baby will enjoy playing with balls. You can sit across from her and roll a ball to her. Encourage her to roll it back. Clap your hands when she does. If the ball is big and soft (like a beach ball), she may be able to try to catch it.

**Finger Walk**     Take a little walk with baby holding on to your finger. Baby can choose to hold on or to let go. Talk to baby about what you see and where you're going. "Let's walk over to those flowers," "Let's walk down the hall," or "You're a good walker!"

**Dance Fever**     Play some fun dancing music, and show baby how to dance! Wiggle and turn, clap, and stomp your feet. Try lots of different kinds of music. Wave around some scarves and ribbons. Have a dance party.

Ages & Stages

**12–16 months**

# Fine Motor
## Activities to Help Your Baby Grow and Learn

Baby is using fingers with more skill now. He will point with his index finger and can pick up tiny bits of cereal with his thumb and finger. He can hold and mark with a crayon or felt-tip pen and grasp small objects such as pegs and insert them in a pegboard.

**Budding Artist**  Let baby draw a picture for you with a crayon and a large piece of paper. Give baby plenty of room. Baby may only make a few marks, but give a lot of praise: "Look at the picture you made!" Be sure to put the crayon away when you both are finished. Your baby doesn't yet know that you only want marks on the paper.

**Ball Toss**  Encourage your child to practice throwing a small, soft ball. Have him stand in one spot and throw the ball. Try again—see how far it goes. At first he may need you to show him how to throw the ball. "Wow, look how far it went!"

**Carton Construction**  Rinse and save pint and quart milk cartons to use for blocks. Show baby how to stack them, then knock them down. Line them up to make a wall, and then knock them down again.

**Tacky Tape**  Make a small wad of masking tape with the sticky side out. Give this to baby to play with. It is very entertaining and will give baby some good finger exercise.

**Squeezing**  Give baby a sponge, washcloth, or sponge ball to play with in the bath. Show baby how to squeeze the water out. You might also let baby play with plastic squirt toys. That's really fun!

**Fill and Dump**  Give baby a plastic container or box and a few items such as a clothespin, a spoon, a toy car, and a spool. Make sure the items are big enough that they do not pose a choking hazard. Show baby how to put them all in the container, then dump them all out again. Tomorrow, change the container or the objects.

**Library Time**  Find a time every 2 weeks or so to go to the library. Pick out new books with your child. Cuddle up every day and read together. Read the story, talk about pictures, and let her take turns turning pages and pointing to pictures. What a special time together!

Ages & Stages

12–16 months

# Problem Solving
## Activities to Help Your Baby Grow and Learn

Your baby is a busy explorer. She enjoys holding, stacking, and playing with toys. She is learning her body parts and can probably point to at least one if you ask her. She enjoys books and will "pat" her favorite picture. She may try to help turn pages in a book. She enjoys learning about how things work.

| | |
|---|---|
| **Money in the Bank** | Make a money bank out of a large can or a plastic container. Cut a long slit in the plastic cover about $1/2$-inch wide. Use the circular ends from frozen juice cans as "money," or cut circles from a box. Show your baby how to put these "coins" into the bank. |
| **Water Painting** | Give your baby a clean paintbrush and a small bucket of plain water. On a sunny day, go outside and let your child paint the walls, sidewalk, or fence with water. Your child will enjoy this "painting." Then you can watch it dry, and paint again. Try this inside with a small paintbrush and a piece of paper. Watch the painting disappear! |
| **Problem Solving** | Let your baby figure out how things work and what they do. Show baby how the switch turns the light on and off. Show him how the flashlight works. Talk to him about what you are doing and why: "I'm putting on a coat because I am cold." |
| **Little Hunter** | During quiet times, ask your baby to find the blanket or get a book from another room. Ask her to get things she cannot see at the time. She might need a little help. When baby is successful, be sure to say, "Thank you." |
| **Matching Game** | Children this age are just beginning to notice when two things are alike, especially shoes, socks, or other objects they know about. Play this game: Hold up one of baby's shoes or a sock. Ask baby, "Where's the other one just like this?" Help baby make the match. "Yes, these two are the same." |
| **Copy Me** | Play a game with your baby. You do something and then try to get baby to imitate you. Clap your hands. If he tries, say, "Look, you can clap, too!" Touch your nose, stick out your tongue, and say, "You try." When he does something new, imitate him. Be silly and have fun. You can also try this with a mirror. |

Ages&Stages

## 12–16 months

# Personal-Social
## Activities to Help Your Baby Grow and Learn

Your sociable baby likes to roll the ball and play Peekaboo or other interactive games with you. He needs to know you are nearby. He actually likes to be the center of attention now! He will show you great affection but may collapse into a tantrum when things don't go his way. He is proud of his new skills, and he wants to learn how to do things by himself.

**Dress-Up** — Your baby may enjoy dressing up in different hats and shoes and looking at herself in the mirror. Make a dress-up box with scarves, ties, and silly masks. Add new things every now and then. You can find great things at thrift shops.

**Help Around the House** — Your baby can help do small jobs such as wiping the table with a sponge, stirring pancake mix (with your help), or sweeping up a little dirt with a small broom. He will enjoy doing something special for you. Be sure to praise him for helping.

**Brushing Teeth** — Give baby her own toothbrush. Let her see you or her siblings brushing their teeth. Put a tiny dab of toothpaste (without fluoride) on the brush (if any) so baby can taste it. Don't expect much brushing; she will probably chew the bristles as she learns about this new thing; and you may need to finish for her. Be sure to put baby's toothbrush in a clean safe place until next time.

**To Market, to Market** — Take baby to the supermarket with you so baby can "help." Talk about all of the colors and smells. Let baby hold something, such as a small can or a lemon. At the checkout, let baby "pay" the cashier. What a good helper!

**Hide-and-Seek** — At home, play Hide-and-Seek by hiding just behind a door, calling to baby, then peeking out so you can be "found." A sibling may have fun playing this game. It helps baby understand that when you disappear, you will come back.

**Bathing Baby** — When bathing baby, let him bathe a small plastic doll. Show baby how to be gentle with the doll. Later, let baby dry and hug the doll. It will teach him to be loving.

**Cleanup Time** — Ask baby to help you put the toys away. You will need a box or a shelf where toys should be placed. Show baby how to pick up the toys and where to put them. What a good helper!

**\*\*\*** Ages&Stages

12–16 months

# Communication
## Activities to Help Your Toddler Grow and Learn

Your toddler is beginning to enjoy language and words. She has many new words now and is beginning to put two words together for simple sentences. She looks at you when you are talking to her, says "hi" and "bye," and points to things she wants. She also enjoys singing and will try to imitate singing favorite songs.

**Chatter Stretchers**  Your toddler may use single words for requests, such as "juice" when he wants a drink. Help him stretch his sentence by saying it for him: "Would you like some juice?" "Say, I want juice, please." Praise him when he attempts to make the sentence longer.

**What Happened Today?**  When you get home from an outing, ask your toddler to tell someone else about what happened or what the two of you saw. "Tell Grandpa about the horse we saw." Help her if you need to, but let her tell as much as she can.

**"Help Me" Game**  Ask your toddler to help you by giving simple directions such as "Help Daddy. Can you get my shoe?" or "It's time to change your diaper. Can you get me a diaper?" You may need to point with your finger to help him in the beginning. Be sure to say, "Thank you. You're such a big help" when he helps.

**Animal Sounds**  Teach your toddler the sounds that animals such as cats, dogs, and cows make. Read books about baby animals, and play with your toddler by making the baby animal sounds. Later, pretend you are the animal's parent and your toddler is the baby animal. Call each other with animal sounds. This game can be a lot of silly fun.

**Read, Read, Read**  Find times to "read" throughout the day. At this age, you can point to pictures and words and your child will begin to learn what words are about. At the grocery store, point to and read signs to your child. At a restaurant, let your child "read" a menu. At home, help her "read" magazines by looking at pictures.

**Junk Box**  Put together a junk box of safe, everyday items that are interesting to explore and feel. Examples of things to put in the box are plastic cups, a soft sock, a scoop from a detergent box, a sponge, and a small shoe. When your child pulls something out of the box, say, "Look, you found a soft blue sock," or "That sponge is squishy." Use new language for your child, and change items in the box every few days.

Ages&Stages

16–20 months

# Gross Motor

## Activities to Help Your Toddler Grow and Learn

By now your active toddler is attempting to run. He can carry large items and toys and loves to push and pull big things such as boxes around on the floor. He's learning how to walk upstairs with one hand held by you and is getting better at walking down stairs. He may climb up into a chair to see and reach new things. Your watchful eye is important.

**Swinging**  Take your child to a park to swing. Be sure the swing is safe and has a seat belt. Show your child how to push her feet out when swinging forward. Push gently so you know baby will hold on. Chant in rhythm while you push: "Up you go, and up you go!"

**Climbing the Stairs**  Hold baby's hand while you climb up steps or a few stairs. Be patient; stairs are very high for little legs. Don't expect much luck with climbing down just yet. If you don't have any stairs in your house or yard, a playground will have places to practice, such as a small slide or a jungle gym platform.

**Balance Beam**  Put a 2-inch wide strip of masking tape on the floor or sidewalk. Let your child walk along the tape, placing one foot in front of the other. Praise your child. Tell him, "You really know how to balance!"

**Chasing**  Your toddler is beginning to run now. In a grassy part of your yard or a safe park, play chase with your little one. Most toddlers love to be chased, and they love to be caught and hugged. Your toddler will love doing this over and over! It's good exercise.

**Moving Day**  Give your child a small wagon or a box with a pull string for hauling toys around. Your child can load the wagon and unload at a different place. Maybe the teddy bear wants to ride!

**Playing Music**  Your toddler will love making and moving to music. A small keyboard or a little tambourine is fun to play with. You can make a drum with an oatmeal container, large plastic containers, and wooden spoons or chopsticks. Join her for a little music making. Take turns making music and dancing and moving to different rhythms.

**Kickball**  Give your child a medium-size ball (6 inches), and show him how to kick it. You can also make a ball from a wad of newspaper taped all around. See how far he can make it go. Kick it and chase it!

Ages&Stages

16–20 months

# Fine Motor

## Activities to Help Your Toddler Grow and Learn

Your toddler is becoming more skillful with hands and fingers. She can play with and use toys in many ways, including stacking, poking, pushing, and pulling. She is also gaining skill at holding and using crayons or felt-tip pens. She knows how to take pieces out of a simple puzzle and will try to put the pieces back together.

**Tear it Up**  After you each wash your hands, show your child how to tear lettuce or spinach leaves into a bowl. Be sure to tell the family who made the salad. (Your child may also like tearing strips of newspaper. Stuff them in a paper bag, tape it up, and make a kick ball.)

**Aim and Drop**  Show your little one how to drop a clothespin or spoon into an open milk carton or other plastic container with a large opening. Play the game as long as your toddler enjoys it. Let him shake the container and enjoy the sound.

**Stacking Blocks**  Let your little one play with wooden cubes or blocks. Show her how to stack them one on top of another. Build a tower. Count aloud as you stack the blocks so that she begins to hear the sound of numbers. She'll love knocking down the tower. Little plastic containers can be washed out and stacked, too.

**String-a-Snack**  Give your toddler a small container of Cheerios or other round cereal and a clean shoelace or a piece of string with tape around the end to make it stiff. Show him how to string the Cheerios. Then eat the Cheerios!

**Place Mats**  Make sure your toddler gets plenty of chances to practice writing and drawing. You might keep paper and washable crayons in the kitchen so you can supervise while getting dinner ready. Use her drawings for place mats for the family. Make sure your little writer knows that writing only happens on the paper.

**Snack Helper**  Let your toddler help make a snack. With your help and supervision, he can unscrew lids from containers such as applesauce or peanut butter. He can help scoop and spread with a plastic knife. He can also help eat. Yummy!

Ages&Stages

16–20 months

# Problem Solving
## Activities to Help Your Toddler Grow and Learn

Your busy learner now recognizes animal pictures and other types of pictures, such as photographs of family members. He enjoys a lot of new activities with your help, such as painting and playing with playdough. He is beginning to understand about things that are similar or that go together in some way. He is very curious about how things work.

**Copy Cat**  On a large piece of paper, draw and scribble together with your toddler. Take turns. You scribble, and then let her scribble. You draw a line, and then let her draw a line. Let her take a turn, and then you copy her scribbles.

**Making Things Fit**  Allow your child a chance to play with puzzles or toys that fit together or inside each other. Plastic containers that "nest" are also fun. Use the word "fit" when you can: "That piece fits in the puzzle."

**Tool Time**  Let your child play games or do tasks in which tools are used. For example, use a sponge to wipe off a chair. Use a strainer to play in the sand. Use measuring cups to fill up containers in the bathtub.

**Match the Socks**  When you fold laundry, set aside some of the socks, both large and small. Show your toddler one sock of a pair, and let him find the other. Show him how to match the socks if he needs help. Ask him, "Whose big blue socks are these?" "Whose little green socks are these?"

**Nature Walk**  Go on a walk in your neighborhood, and collect little things such as rocks and leaves in a small pail or plastic tub. When you get home, try to put things together into different groups. For example, help your child sort big and little rocks, rocks from leaves, or black rocks from white rocks, making sure your toddler doesn't put anything in her mouth. Your child will learn about grouping things.

**Matching Pictures**  Cut out pictures of toys, food, and other familiar objects, and glue them on cards. Have your child try to match cards to actual objects or vice versa. Show your child a picture of a toothbrush. Ask him, "Where is a toothbrush like this?" Then show him a picture of a chair. "Can you find something like this?"

Ages&Stages

16–20 months

# Personal-Social
## Activities to Help Your Toddler Grow and Learn

Your toddler is gaining more independence every day. She may show jealousy of others who get attention, especially siblings. She is very interested in other children. She likes to do things by herself and may become a little bossy and resist your suggestions. Your good humor will go far in seeing you both through the coming months.

**Big Time Mealtime**  Let your toddler join the family at the table for meals and eat with his own spoon and fork. He may need a booster seat to be right at the table. He can begin to drink from a small plastic cup (just don't fill it to the top). He can even help you set a place at the table. Talk about what a big boy and good helper he is.

**Family Dancing**  Show your toddler how to dance. Play music, and show her how to imitate you or dance with you. Invite other family members to dance along. Pick up your toddler and dance with her. Praise your little one. Give her a hug.

**Storytime**  This is a good time to establish the habit of reading stories every night before bed. After brushing teeth and getting ready for bed, cuddle up and enjoy a favorite book. It is especially good to read with the TV turned off. This might also be a special time for another member of the family to share with your toddler.

**Comfort Me**  Because your toddler is so busy and is often frustrated, he will need a lot of comfort and reassurance. He responds to what he's feeling right now and cannot really understand that he will feel better in just a little while. He will need your warm voice, a hug, and comfort.

**Tickles and Kisses**  While getting your toddler ready for bed, say goodnight with a little tickle or kiss to different parts of baby: "Goodnight little nose (tickle), goodnight little foot (tickle), goodnight little ear (tickle)." Ask your baby what part needs a goodnight tickle or a goodnight kiss.

Ages&Stages

16–20 months

# Communication

## Activities to Help Your Toddler Grow and Learn

Your toddler is learning language very quickly and will imitate what he hears, good or bad. He is using different types of words and putting them together in short phrases. Most of his words are understandable. He is starting to sing simple songs.

**Sock Puppet**
Put your hand in a clean sock and make it talk. "Hi, my name is Joe. I am visiting you. What is your name?" Your child might say something or want to touch the puppet. Keep the conversation going.

**Construction Time**
Collect materials to make a pretend airport, street, or neighborhood. Masking tape can be the runway or the road. Oatmeal containers can be tunnels. Cereal boxes can be buildings. Cardboard can make a ramp for cars to go up and down. Toy cars can go through the tunnel, under the bridge, or down a ramp. Use new words while your child plays.

**Following Directions**
As you talk to your child, begin to give simple directions such as "Bring me the blue sock," or "Put your doll on the chair." At first, you might have to show your child what is blue or what "on the chair" means. Offer a lot of praise. Another game you can play is Show Me. You say, "Show me the door," and your child touches the door. Good job!

**Fun with Books**
Find large picture books and/or magazines to look at with your child. Point to pictures and talk about what you see. Ask him, "Where's the doggie?" and have him point to a picture. Let your child "read" to someone else, like Grandpa. If your child is beginning to learn about using the toilet, this is a good time to put a small basket of potty-related books in the bathroom for him to "read."

**Field Trips**
Your toddler will enjoy going to new places, even to a new store. This is a great time to learn new words. Talk to her about what you are seeing. "Look, that fruit is called a kiwi." "Look at that big fountain."

**Sing a Song**
Your child will love learning simple songs such as Twinkle, Twinkle, Little Star. Teach your child this song or a simple song you remember from childhood. Enjoy singing together. Later, ask your child to sing for someone else in the family.

Ages&Stages

20–24 months

# Gross Motor

## Activities to Help Your Toddler Grow and Learn

Your toddler is busy and fast! She is running and learning to kick and jump. Her leg muscles are getting stronger, and she can walk up and down stairs holding on to your hand or a railing. She really enjoys moving her body and learning new skills.

**Froggie Jump**
Hold your child's hands and help him jump off a low step. Then let him try it by himself. Once he can do this, show your child how to jump over something such as a small milk carton. Encourage your child: "Wow! You can jump just like a froggie."

**Bowling Adventure**
Show your child how to roll a large ball toward "pins" to knock them down. Balls can be made from large wads of newspaper taped all around. Empty milk cartons or plastic soda bottles can be used for "pins." When your child gets tired of bowling, you can play kickball.

**Balancing Act**
Assist your child by holding her hand, and ask her to stand on one foot. Then ask her to stand on the other foot. Now see if she can stand without holding your hand. Count how many seconds she can balance. Keep practicing.

**Let's Go for a Ride**
Give your child a riding toy with pedals. It will help him control the movement of the toy and strengthen his legs. Later he will enjoy riding a tricycle with pedals.

**Dance Party**
Play different kinds of music: rock and roll, country, classical, and ethnic music—any that you and your child enjoy. Dance and move to the music with your child. Allow her to move freely as she listens. Sometimes pick her up so she can feel you move. Mostly, let her dance and move by herself. She may enjoy dancing with scarves or ribbons.

**Trip to the Playground**
Find a playground in your neighborhood, and have some fun! Run, swing, and climb. As you walk to the playground, practice stepping up or down street curbs holding your child's hand. Encourage him to walk up stairs by holding on to the railing.

Ages&Stages

20–24 months

# Fine Motor

## Activities to Help Your Toddler Grow and Learn

Your busy toddler enjoys quiet activities that build small muscles. He can stack and build with small toys. He is learning how to hold a crayon with his thumb and fingers and how to make circular and horizontal scribbles. He is becoming more skillful at stringing beads and doing other activities that require working with two hands.

**Stack it Up**  Your child will have fun stacking small things and knocking them down. Use blocks, film containers, spools of thread, or anything stackable. Count how many things your child can stack. See how high she can go!

**String Fling**  String beads, macaroni, or large cereal, and help your child practice using two hands at one time. A shoelace or string with some tape on the end will work well for stringing. Make necklaces and bracelets.

**Family Book**  Make a small picture album for your toddler. Include pictures of family members, friends, and pets. Look through the album and talk about each person. Have him turn pages and tell you about the pictures. Have him share his special book with visitors.

**Beginning Puzzles**  Show baby how to put beginning puzzles together. You can make a puzzle by cutting the front of a cereal box into two or three wide strips. Help her turn the piece if she needs help. Praise her for trying. Tell her, "Good for you! You can do it!"

**Letters and Shopping Lists**  When you make out your shopping list or write letters, have paper and a pen or crayon for your child to write along with you. "I'm writing a letter to Grandma. You can write one, too." Send the letters in the mail. Grandma may write back!

**Make Fruit Salad**  Let your child use a Popsicle stick or a plastic picnic knife to help you cut bits of fruit such as banana or peaches. He can help scoop yogurt, sprinkle in nuts or raisins, and stir everything together. Don't forget to tell the family who made the salad.

**PB and J**  Your child will enjoy making her own snack. She can help twist open lids on jars, open containers, spread peanut butter or jelly, scoop out applesauce, and more. The more she can do herself (with your supervision), the faster she will learn and the more skilled she will become.

**✱✱✱ Ages&Stages**

## 20–24 months

Your toddler is curious about body parts and what they do. She understands more about how things go together, such as where items belong. She knows that a picture of a cat represents a real cat, and she is learning what objects are used for. Her busy mind is trying to make sense of what she sees and experiences.

**Scoop and Pour**   Let your child experience pouring and filling. Provide a lot of recycled materials such as clean milk cartons, yogurt cups, detergent scoops, film containers, and plastic soda bottles for playing in the sand. At home, use uncooked rice or popcorn in a large tray or box and provide scoops and containers. Talk about what your child is doing and use new words such as "empty," "full," "pouring," and "scooping."

**Pretending with Household Objects**   For pretend play, make a box with household tools—such as a flashlight, paintbrushes, a small shovel, or a broom—for your child. Your child can pretend to paint the walls, dig in the garden, or clean up the house. Talk about the purpose of the items: "Flashlights help us see things in the dark."

**I Can Do, Can You?**   During bath time or lap time with your child, play I Can Do, Can You? "My eyes blink; can your eyes blink?" "My nose can sniff; can your nose sniff?" "I can clap my hands. Show me you can clap, too." Do something silly. This game is a lot of fun.

**Make-Believe Play**   Make a cooking box with an apron, pots, spoons, and bowls, or make a doctor bag using a makeup bag with a play stethoscope (old earphones are good), bandages, Popsicle sticks for tongue depressors, a clipboard and/or file folders, and a white dress shirt. Take these out for some special make-believe play. Have a mirror nearby.

**Topsy Turvy**   Turn things (books, cups, a box of cereal) upside down and see if your child notices and turns them back the right way. Have fun with this silly game.

**Railroad Tracks**   While your child is watching, draw two long horizontal lines about 4 inches apart on a large sheet of paper. Then, show your child how to draw vertical lines from one to the other. Encourage him to make a lot of these vertical lines. The design will look like a railroad track. Bring out the trains or cars to play on the railroad track.

Ages & Stages

20–24 months

# Personal-Social

## Activities to Help Your Toddler Grow and Learn

Your toddler is beginning to exercise his newly found independence. He will want to do everything by himself, even if he cannot. He wants things now and quickly becomes frustrated if that doesn't happen. He will enjoy playing alongside other children even though he is not really able to share just yet. He likes to imitate simple household tasks and can put some of his toys away with some help from you.

**Baby Bear Beds**    Make a little bed for your child's doll or a stuffed animal from a shoebox. A small piece of cloth or a dishtowel makes a blanket or a pillow. Your child can help her baby go to bed at night. She can read a story and tuck him into his new bed. Don't forget a kiss.

**Play Dates**    Your child will need your help in playing with others but enjoys being with other children. Stay close by when he is with other children. Having a lot of the same kinds of toys helps the children cooperate. Several trucks, cars, and dolls are easier to share than one of each kind. Praise children for playing well together.

**Dress-Up**    Make a box with dress-up clothing. Your child will have a lot of fun pretending. Have a bag or box with dress-up items: hats, scarves, shoes, old jewelry, and a wallet. Add clothing with large buttons and zippers to practice buttoning and zipping. Your child will need some help, but soon she will be able to get dressed all by herself. Give her a lot of praise for her efforts. Don't forget to let her look in the mirror.

**Playing House**    Place a plastic dishpan on a low table for doing dishes. Add a doll, plastic plates, cups, and some cooking utensils. Make playhouse furniture for your child. Turn a box over, and draw the burners to make a stove. Follow your child's lead; talk and have fun.

**Picnic Outing**    Find a place to have a picnic with your child. A park or the playground is a fun place, but your child will have fun even if the picnic is just in the living room. Let your child help prepare some simple food and drinks for the picnic. Maybe the stuffed animals would like to join you. Let your child practice eating all by himself.

Ages&Stages

20–24 months

# Communication
## Activities to Help Your Toddler Grow and Learn

Your toddler enjoys being with you and is learning new words very quickly. She is using her language more often to let you know her wants, needs, and ideas. She can carry on a simple conversation and may talk to herself or pretend to have a conversation with a stuffed animal. She can follow simple directions and loves to read books. She likes to hear the same book read over and over!

**I Spy**
In the car or on the bus, you can play "I Spy." You say, "I spy with my eye a green truck." Then your child tries to find what you spied. Now it is his turn to spy something. Remember to "spy" things your child can see from his car seat. You might also try "I hear with my ear." Listen for sounds such as a motorcycle, a car horn, a bird singing, a dog barking, or a radio.

**Picture Album**
Make a little picture album with pictures of your child and people and pets he knows. Have your child talk about the pictures and name the people and pets. Ask your child, "Who's that?" "What are they doing?" Look at this book over and over. Help your child learn to say her first and last name.

**When You Were Little**
Tell your child stories about when he was little: "When you were first born..." or "When you were a little baby..." Your child will love to hear these stories again and again.

**Dinner Report**
At the end of a busy day, let everyone talk about his or her day. Ask your child to tell others in the family what she did during the day. Let her take her time. You might remind her if she forgets some events. Soon she will learn to tell what happened in the right order. Praise her for remembering so much.

**Washing a Baby**
Let your child wash a baby doll in a plastic tub, or bring a baby doll into his bath with him. Name the doll's body parts as he washes the baby: "You're washing the baby's feet." Praise your child for taking such good care of his baby.

**What's that Sound?**
Turn off the TV and radio, and listen with your child to sounds around the house. Listen to the refrigerator motor, wind chimes, a clock ticking, or people talking. Ask your child to tell you what she hears. Try this at night. Listen for the night sounds of crickets and frogs.

Ages & Stages

24–30 months

# Gross Motor
## Activities to Help Your Toddler Grow and Learn

The word "active" still best describes your toddler. His muscles are getter stronger. He is gaining more confidence with his abilities. Allow your toddler to continue physical activities he enjoys, such as kicking balls, riding toys, climbing jungle gyms, swinging, running, jumping, and balancing.

**Copy Cat** — Stand on one foot. Ask your child "Can you do this?" If your child stands only for one second, praise her. Pretend to be an airplane flying with your arms out across the room. Try other movements; jump, crawl, gallop, and tiptoe around the house. Let your child be the leader and copy her. Play with the whole family.

**Jumping Frog Contest** — Pretend you and your child are frogs or kangaroos and jump with both feet together. Show your child how to jump with both feet together, and then jump over a chalk line or a small object such as a washcloth. Make marks with the chalk to measure how far he can jump with both feet together. Comment to your child, "Wow, look how far the frog jumped that time!"

**Soccer Star** — Play "soccer" with your child. Use a medium-size ball (8–10 inches) and set up a goal with two empty milk cartons or a large cardboard box turned on its side. Encourage your child to kick the ball through the cartons or into the box. Great goal!

**Playground Fun** — Just about every day is a good day to spend some time outside in the yard or on a playground. Encourage your child to run, swing, and climb up play structures and slide down slides. Join your child in these activities. If you walk to the playground, jump over cracks or sticks on the way. Help your child to practice stepping up and down stairs or jumping down from short steps. Meet other children and parents. Have a great time!

**Basketball Hoops** — Practice bouncing, catching, and throwing a medium-size ball. You can use a garbage can or laundry basket for a target and can celebrate when your child "makes a basket." Help your child learn how to catch by showing her how to hold out her hands to catch the ball. Start by standing really close together so that she can have more success.

**Horsing Around** — Play Ride the Horse and bounce you toddler on your knees or hold his hands as he straddles your foot and let him ride your foot. (Crossing your legs makes it less tiring to bounce him.) Stop bouncing every now and then, and wait for him to bounce or ask for more. Ask your child, "More? You want to ride some more?"

**✱✱✱ Ages&Stages**

24–30 months

# Fine Motor

## Activities to Help Your Toddler Grow and Learn

Your toddler's eyes and hands are working together well. He enjoys taking apart and putting small things together. He loves using any kind of "writing" or drawing tool. Enjoy the time together by providing plenty of scratch paper, washable crayons and marking pens, and so forth. Allow writing and drawing to take place at a table while you supervise so that your artist will not draw on walls or furniture. Provide puzzles, blocks, and other safe small toys and plenty of conversation.

| | |
|---|---|
| **Flipping Pancakes** | Trim the corners from an ordinary household sponge to form a "pancake." Give your child a small skillet and a spatula. Show him how to flip the pancake. |
| **Macaroni String** | String a necklace out of macaroni (tube-shape pasta, such as rigatoni, works really well). Your child can paint the pasta before or after stringing it. Make sure she has a string with a stiff tip, such as a shoelace. You can use yarn, but tape the ends so that it is easy to string. |
| **Homemade Orange Juice** | Make orange juice or lemonade with your toddler. Have him help squeeze the fruit using a handheld juicer. To make lemonade, you will need to add some sugar and water. Show your toddler how to twist the fruit back and forth on the squeezer to get the juice out. Cheers! |
| **Copy Me** | Have your child copy a line that you draw, up and down and side to side. You take a turn and then your child takes a turn. Try zigzag patterns, then spirals. Use a crayon and paper, a stick in the sand, markers on newspaper, or your fingers on a steamy bathroom mirror. |
| **Bath-Time Fun** | While bathing your toddler, let her play with things to squeeze, such as a sponge, a washcloth, or a squeeze toy. Squeezing really helps strengthen the muscles in her hands and fingers. Besides, it makes bath time more fun! |
| **My Favorite Things** | Your child can make a book about all of his favorite things. Clip or staple a few pieces of paper together for him. (Let him choose his favorite color.) Help him use safety scissors to cut pictures out of magazines and glue them on the pages. He can use markers or crayons to decorate pages and to try to write his name. Write down what he says about each page. Stickers can be fun to put in this book, too. |
| **Sorting Objects** | Find a divided plate (e.g., a TV dinner tray). Into a plastic bowl, put some common objects such as nuts, shells, and coins. Let your toddler use a spoon or tongs to pick up the objects and put them in different sections of the plate. Make sure you watch your child with small objects to make sure she doesn't put them in her mouth. |

**＊＊＊ Ages&Stages**

24–30 months

# Problem Solving
## Activities to Help Your Toddler Grow and Learn

Doing things all by herself is very important for your toddler. Be patient and enjoy this time of growing independence, even though it may sometimes be frustrating. Give your child plenty of time and chances to figure out and do things by herself. Make-believe is also an important part of your toddler's growth; real and make-believe can be confusing. Help your child learn about the difference, especially when watching TV.

| | |
|---|---|
| **Paper Bag Matching Game** | Gather at least two of several household objects. Use two paper bags with the same things in each bag. Pull one item out and ask your child to reach in and find one in his bag. Remind your child, "No peeking, just feeling!" |
| **Helping Around the House** | Ask your toddler to help with the laundry. Sort things by color, or gather only white things. Maybe all of the baby clothes go in one place. Let your child help you put all of the socks in one pile and all of the shirts in another. She can line up the shoes and boots in the right place, and you can help her make sure they are in pairs. |
| **Snack-Time Roundup** | When giving a snack to your child, teach him how to line up pieces of fruit, small crackers, or cereal loops. You can make a line of four things, and have him copy you. You can help your toddler count the food pieces and then eat them up. |
| **Building with Boxes** | Gather up several small and medium-size boxes to use as building blocks. You can use shoe boxes, cereal boxes, clean milk cartons, and so forth. Encourage your child to build with the boxes. Ask her, "What are you making?" "Is that a house?" "Is it a wall?" Add toy cars or animals for more fun. |
| **Where Is it?** | Using any object in your house, play Where Is It? with your toddler. For example, hide a stuffed bear under the pillow. Give your toddler clues to find the bear: "Where's bear? Can you find her? She's under something green," or "She is behind something soft." Give your toddler help as needed, and then let him hide things and give you some clues. |

Ages&Stages

24–30 months

Your toddler is still working on doing things for himself and wants very much to please adults. He enjoys feeding himself and dressing himself without your help. Since toddlers love to imitate, you can let him help around the house with simple tasks, such as wiping up spills. Your extra support and patience will make life easier for both of you, especially if there's a new baby at home.

| | |
|---|---|
| **Dapper Dresser** | Taking off clothing is probably easy for your child. Now begin having her put on her own clothes. Start with loose-fitting shorts. Have her sit on the floor, put both legs in the shorts, stand up, and then pull up shorts. Tell your child, "Wow! You put those on all by yourself!" Let her look at herself in a mirror. Now practice putting on a T-shirt: head first ("Boo!"), then one arm, and then the other arm. "What an excellent dresser you are!" |
| **Playmates** | Invite a one of your child's friends over to play for a short period of time, or take your child to a relative's house where there is someone his age. Make sure there are enough toys to play with to share easily. Later, let him tell you all about his experience. |
| **First Feelings** | Help your child name feelings when they happen. When your child is worried, you can help her understand the feeling by telling her, "You look worried. Can you tell me about it?" If you know your child is frustrated, use the words: "I know you are really frustrated, but you can have a turn in a minute." When your child learns that feelings have names, she will be able to handle them more easily. |
| **Holding a Baby** | Let your child hold a baby, either a sibling or a relative or neighbor's baby (with their permission). Supervise your child as he holds the baby, and help him sit steadily and hold his arms appropriately for support. Talk about how babies must be handled gently. Tell him what a good friend he is to baby and how baby likes him. |
| **All by Myself** | Enjoy a meal during which your little one feeds herself using a fork. Mashed potatoes will be a little easier than peas, but soon your little one will have mastered peas, too! Show her how to twist noodles. Better have an extra napkin on hand! |
| **Big Little Parent** | When your toddler plays with a doll or teddy bear, give him a small plastic dish, a spoon, and a cup. He may also need a baby blanket and maybe a hairbrush and toothbrush. Now he can really take care of that baby bear! |

Ages&Stages

24–30 months

# Communication

## Activities to Help Your Toddler Grow and Learn

Your child can talk about many things and can follow simple directions. She will make mistakes with her grammar, saying "foots" instead of "feet," for example. Your child can tell you what's happening. She's using longer sentences now. Talk about what happened during the day. Read to your child every day. She might even pretend to read favorite books by herself, using the words you have read to her.

**Reading Magazines**  Talk about the pictures in ordinary household magazines. Find pictures of household items that your child will recognize, such as toothpaste, soap, diapers, pets, or cars. Point to the picture and ask, "What is this?" "Do we have this at home?"

**Silly Me**  Your child will have fun if you pretend you don't know what things really are. Point to the toothpaste and ask your child, "Is that the soap?" Let him tell you what it really is. Act surprised. Your child will enjoy "teaching" you the right name of things.

**Bandage Game**  Make pretend bandages using tape or stickers. Ask your child, "Where is your cut? Where shall I put this?" Get your child to name as many body parts as possible, and put a bandage on each part. You can wash the bandage off during bath time. This game can also be played with a doll or stuffed animal.

**Let's Put Things Away**  When putting away food after going to the market or putting away gardening tools after planting seeds, ask your child to help. Tell her, "Put the butter in the refrigerator" or "Put the shovel in the pail." You'll have fun giving some silly directions, too, such as "Put the lemons under the chair." Use words such as "up" and "down."

**What's Going On?**  When reading books or magazines, ask your child to tell you what's happening in a picture: "What's the baby doing?" "What is the dog doing?" Then, listen carefully to your child's interesting story.

**What's Your Name?**  Play this silly name game. When you greet your child, act as if you don't know who he is. Say, "Hello, little boy. What's your name?" When he tells you, greet him with happy surprise. "Oh, you're my little boy! I'm so happy to see you!"

Ages & Stages

30–36 months

# Gross Motor
## Activities to Help Your Toddler Grow and Learn

Your child is improving skills using his leg and arm muscles. He is working on making these muscles stronger, more flexible, more coordinated, and quicker. He can catch an 8-inch ball, jump about 2 feet, make sharp turns around a corner while running, and avoid obstacles in his path.

**Over the River**  When playing outside, place a small towel or piece of cloth about 24 inches wide on the grass. This is the "river." Have your child run and jump over the river without getting wet. At first, you can bunch the towel up in the middle or fold it so that the river is only about 12 inches wide. As your child is able, you can open the towel so that the river is wider.

**Balloon Kick**  Let your child kick a balloon from one end of the room to another. Lay a box on its side for a goal. See if she can kick the balloon into the box.

**Animal Walk**  Show your child how to walk like different animals (e.g., squat like a duck, walk on all fours like a dog). Encourage him to pretend to be these animals and make noises like them. Play along. Call the cat: "Here, kitty, kitty." Balance on one foot like a flamingo.

**Heel-to-Toe Walk**  Show your child how to walk heel to toe using a line on the sidewalk or a short length of clothesline on the ground. Show your child how to outstretch her arms to keep her balance.

**Basketball**  Place an empty laundry basket on the floor against an empty wall. Give your child a soft ball about 4 inches in size. Place a string or piece of tape on the floor for a throw-line, and show your child how to throw overhand to get the ball in the basket. Start about 4 feet back from the basket. Move back as your child gets better.

**Chasing Bubbles**  On a nice day, while playing outside, blow bubbles and ask your child to clap his hands together and pop them. Blow some high so that your child can jump up. Blow some far away from you so that your child will need to dash out a little. Clap all of the big ones. Now, clap and pop all of the little ones. Play this game as long as you both enjoy it. When you're done, go wash those soapy hands together!

Ages&Stages

30–36 months

# Fine Motor

## Activities to Help Your Toddler Grow and Learn

Your child is learning to hold pens, crayons, and markers with her thumb and two fingers just like big people do. She has learned to make scissors open and close and can make snips in paper when you hold it. She can string beads easily and can work puzzles with four or five pieces.

**Yummy Puzzles**  Cut off the front part of your child's favorite cereal box. Now cut this into four or five puzzle pieces. Your child will have fun putting this simple puzzle together. He may need a little help at first.

**Copy Me**  Show your child how to make lines and circles. You might also try simple shapes. Circles and straight lines will be easiest for your child to copy. Your child may want to learn to write the first letter of her name when you are playing this game. Keep it fun. Celebrate any attempt at writing a letter, even if it doesn't look much like the real thing.

**Tong Time**  Give your child a pair of small kitchen tongs or ice tongs. See if he can move cotton balls from one container into another. Then try something heavier such as walnuts, spools, or small stones.

**Junior Mechanic**  Collect large bolts, matching nuts, and even washers. Your child will enjoy matching the bolt to the nut and twisting them together. Watch your child to be sure she doesn't put anything in her mouth.

**Little Beader**  Have fun stringing large buttons, beads, large pasta tubes (e.g., macaroni, rigatoni), or large loop-shaped cereal. Make sure the string, shoelace, or yarn your child is using has a stiff end; wrap tape around the ends of string to make it easy for beading. Let your child make a necklace for you and one for him. What concentration!

**Bubbles on Paper**  Let your child use a washable crayon or felt-tip pen to draw bubbles on paper. Show her how to draw big bubbles and little bubbles, purple bubbles and green bubbles. Let her draw as many as she wants. Now that she has drawn so many bubbles, maybe it's time to blow some real bubbles!

Ages & Stages

30–36 months

# Problem Solving

## Activities to Help Your Toddler Grow and Learn

Your child can notice similarities and differences among many things. He knows about long and short, a little and a lot, and which one of your kitchen spoons is the biggest. With your help he can put three things of different sizes in order from small to large. Pretend play is still very important and fun for both of you!

**What Is This?**  After giving your child a bath, stand or seat your child in front of a mirror. With a towel, dry different parts of her body. While drying her hair, ask (with a smile and pretend puzzlement), "What is this stuff?" While drying her shoulder ask, "What is this thing?" While drying ribs ask, "What are these bony things?" Have fun being together while tickling, cuddling, and teaching the names of body parts.

**Copycat Cars**  Line up four to five small cars or other objects in a row. Make sure your child sees what you did. Give your child some objects to line up in a row just like you did. You can line up different things, such as blocks, spoons, or shells. Even if your child doesn't do it exactly like you, help out. Say, "See, the red one is by the yellow one." Then, praise your child for playing the game: "Wow, you're a good liner-upper!"

**Big and Little**  Show your child two items of different sizes, such as shoes, cups, or spoons. Ask him to point to the big one, then the little one. You can play Big and Little with many things such as dogs, leaves, and cars, especially at the park. Play this game anywhere in the house or at the supermarket with vegetables, boxes, or cans. Add a medium-size item and change the game to Big, Little, and One in the Middle.

**Tell Me Your Story**  Give your child some plain paper and a few washable crayons or felt-tip pens for drawing. When your child finishes, ask her to tell you about what she drew. Write the story on your child's paper. Print her name. Tell her, "This is your story, and this is your name." Read the story to Grandma or someone else important.

**Reading the Neighborhood**  As you walk or drive around your neighborhood, show your child signs such as the large yellow "M" for McDonald's. Show him a stop sign and tell him what it says. Next time you go out, ask him to read signs with you.

**Silly Sounds**  Play a silly copy game with your child while you are in the car or on the bus. For example, tell her, "Bee, zim, zop" or some other silly phrase. See if your child can copy you. Let your child make up a silly phrase and copy her.

Ages&Stages

30–36 months

*Ages & Stages Learning Activities* by Elizabeth Twombly and Ginger Fink. Copyright © 2004 by Paul H. Brookes Publishing Co. All rights reserved.

# Personal-Social
## Activities to Help Your Toddler Grow and Learn

Your child is becoming more independent in taking care of her personal needs, but she still needs your hugs and reassurance. Usually she can separate from you in familiar settings. She can obey simple rules. She enjoys simple games with other children and takes pride in her accomplishments. She will respond with pride when you notice positive behavior, such as being helpful, following a rule, or doing something for herself.

**Kitchen Helper**    Let your child help with cooking by measuring, pouring, stirring, cutting (with cookie cutters or plastic knives), and tearing salad greens. These are real activities that help the family. Tell him, "Thank you for helping."

**Super Picker-Upper**    Show your child how to put trash in the trash can. If your child drops paper, ask her to pick it up and put it into the trash can. She may enjoy helping you put the can outside for the garbage truck to pick up. Show your child how important it is to keep the world clean. Talk about what would happen if people didn't pick up trash.

**Bathing Beauty**    Your child will enjoy trying to wash himself in the bathtub. Show him how to use a washcloth and soap. Be sure to let your child know that he is doing a good job. Then, give your child a towel so that he can dry himself. Have fun with your child; say, "Whose clean little boy is this?"

**Naming Feelings**    Help your child understand feelings by noticing them and giving them names. Children need to learn that feelings change and that others may have feelings, too. Say, "I can tell you're excited because it's almost your birthday!" Don't be afraid to use big words.

**Super Driver**    Make an obstacle course in the driveway or yard. Let your little driver push a cart or pull a wagon, steering around a box or a flower pot or over a hose. There's a big hug at the finish line!

**Look at You**    Start a dress-up bin for your child. Go through your closet and instead of getting rid of your old clothes, put some of them in a box for your child to play with. Old purses, wallets, hats, ties, shoes, belts, and necklaces are fun. Let your child dress up and then let her look in the mirror. Have your camera ready.

Ages & Stages

30–36 months

# Communication

## Activities to Help Your Child Grow and Learn

Your child is learning to use complete sentences to tell you all about what's happening. He also can follow more than one direction at a time. He has probably learned both his first and last name and can tell you if you ask. He loves to have conversations with a friend or maybe a toy doll or bear. He has learned that a voice on the telephone really comes from a person, even though he can't see the speaker at the time, and your child is more likely to talk than just listen.

**Good Night Everywhere**  When it's time to go to bed, give good-night kisses all over. Tell your child, "I'm going to kiss you under your arm. I'm going to kiss you on top of your head. Now I'm going to kiss you behind your ear. Good night back there! Good night everywhere!"

**Who's This Person?**  Pretend you suddenly forgot who your child is. Say, "What's your name little girl? Is it Samantha? Is it Rosita? Do you have another name?" (When she tells you her name, you can be very happily surprised!)

**Love Notes**  Write little notes to your child and place them here and there during the day. A note might say, "You are a very helpful brother to your baby sister. She thinks you are really special." A note on your child's toy shelf can say you noticed that the toys were put away. A note by the plate at dinnertime can say that Dad will read his favorite story at bedtime. As you read these notes to your little one, he learns that reading is fun and important.

**Where the Creatures Live**  Help your child learn directions by asking, "Where do birds fly? Up in the sky. Where do the bugs live? Under a rock. Where do fish swim? Deep down in the water." Your child may need a little help at first, but soon she will know the answers.

**Weather Person**  At the start of the day, ask your child to look out the window and tell you about the weather. Is it sunny? Is it raining? Is it cloudy? What will the weather be today? Have your child draw a picture of the sun if the day is sunny, raindrops if the day is rainy, and clouds if the sky is cloudy.

**A Card of Love**  Collect pictures of favorite things and animals, plus some stickers, bits of lace, buttons, and other small craft items. You will also need some pieces of paper and glue. Make a Happy Birthday card for someone special, or a Get Well card. While making the card, talk about how special your friend or relative is. Help your child write a message. Address the card, stamp it, and mail it. This little kindness will bring much appreciation.

Ages&Stages

36–42 months

# Gross Motor
## Activities to Help Your Child Grow and Learn

Your child can usually kick a ball forward, jump, and perhaps hop on one foot. She likes to do things for longer periods of time now and may spend quite a long time riding a tricycle or pulling things in a wagon. Climbing is getting to be one of her favorite activities. She also enjoys vigorous play with friends. Having used up all that energy, she will usually sleep well through the night.

**Marching in the Band**  Show your child how to march like a member of the band. Be sure to get those knees up high! Invite a friend to join you. Add a drum and a flag and make a parade!

**Kangaroo Kid**  Show your child how the kangaroo jumps around. Pretend to be a mother kangaroo. With your feet together, jump, jump, jump. This is also a lot of fun outdoors or with a friend.

**Freeze Game**  Play the freeze game. Let your child dance or move around in any way he wants, but when you say "freeze," he has to stop right away in the middle of a motion. You can start the movement up again by saying "melt." Take turns playing this silly game.

**Football Fun**  Give your child a medium-size ball. Show her how to kick it by swinging a foot back, then forward. Turn a cardboard box on its side and encourage your child to kick the ball into the box for a goal. Shout "goal!" when your child gets the ball into the box.

**Airplanes Everywhere**  Let your child pretend to be an airplane and run with his arms outstretched. Show him how to lean to the left, then to the right. Make some airplane noises. Swoop down low and then fly around in a circle. Time to slow down; bend down and land.

**Big Box Basketball**  Place an open box or laundry basket on a tabletop or surface higher than chair level. Give your child a medium-size ball to throw overhand into the box or basket. You can also tie a ribbon across the tops of two chair backs with the box on the other side. Show your child how to throw the ball over the ribbon and into the box.

Ages&Stages

36–42 months

# Fine Motor

## Activities to Help Your Child Grow and Learn

Your child is becoming more skilled at buttoning and zipping clothing. He can use a fork and spoon to feed himself. He can spread soft butter on bread. He can hold a pencil or crayon with his thumb and two fingers and likes to draw. When asked, he may be able to draw circles or other simple marks.

**Button-Up Bear** — Let your child dress a large stuffed teddy bear or large doll with real baby clothing. Make sure the baby clothes have a couple of large buttons or snaps to let your child practice small finger work. You might even find some baby shoes with Velcro closures. Tying or buckling shoes is probably too difficult right now.

**Beautiful Necklace** — Cut some circles or flowers out of colored paper, and punch a hole in the center. Then, cut a large plastic soda straw into pieces. Let your child string a shoelace with alternating flowers and straw pieces. She probably will not always alternate pieces, but that doesn't matter. Tie the ends, and she will have her own beautiful necklace!

**Picking Peas** — Buy a few fresh peapods at the market. Show your child how to find the peas inside the shell. Give him a few in a plastic container to shell for himself. When he is finished, rinse off the peas and eat them. Yum!

**Sidewalk Artist** — Let your child draw pictures on the sidewalk or driveway with colored outdoor chalk. If you don't have chalk, give your child a small paintbrush and let her paint a picture with water. The painting will be fun, and so will the magic of evaporation. "Where did your picture go?"

**List Maker** — Keep a small pad of paper and a few pencils close at hand. Before going shopping, ask your child to help you make a shopping list. Let him write his own version of words and see if he can remember what they mean. He can also write a note to his Mom or a pet.

**Little Snipper** — Let your child practice cutting with safety scissors. Show her how to open and close the scissors while you hold the paper. Later, show her how to hold the scissors with one hand and the paper in the other. At first, just snipping the edge is great progress. If she snips off a few pieces, save them in an envelope. Later you can paste the pieces on a sheet of paper for a special art creation!

Ages&Stages

36–42 months

# Problem Solving

## Activities to Help Your Child Grow and Learn

Your busy learner is gaining many skills. She can put puzzles together (six pieces or maybe more), draw some shapes, such as circles and squares, and identify a few colors. She can match an object to a picture of that object and notices many similarities and differences. She is very curious about how things work, and your answers really help her understand and learn.

**Box o' Blocks**   Collect blocks and small boxes for your child to use for building. Make something and let him copy what you build. Add pieces of cardboard for a roof and some paint stirring sticks for bridges. Make a town. Add some toy cars and toy people; the town will come to life!

**Memory Magic**   Play this game to help your child develop her memory. In a car or on a bus, tell your child, "We're going on a picnic, and we're bringing a..." Name an object that you would bring on a picnic, such as an apple. Encourage your child to think of another object to bring on a picnic and repeat "We're going on a picnic, and we're bringing...," then name your object (apple) followed by hers (balloon). Take turns thinking of what to bring on a picnic, each time repeating what has already been named. Try to name things alphabetically.

**Mr. Sticks**   Ask your child to draw a stick figure about 5 inches tall on a paper plate or piece of cardboard. Say, "This is Mr. Sticks." Now, hide Mr. Sticks. Give your child clues to lead him to Mr. Sticks: "He's in a room with water, but not the bathroom." "He's in a drawer near a door." Finding Mr. Sticks earns a big hug. Now it's your child's turn to give you clues.

**Money Management**   Make some play dollar bills from green paper. Put them in an old purse or wallet for your child. Pretend to be the storekeeper. Say, "Those socks cost $2.00." "This lunch costs $3.00." Help your child count the right amount of money. Now change places. Let your child be the storekeeper. Add to the fun by collecting cereal boxes, empty milk cartons, and plastic juice cans to make a store.

**Picture Shopping List**   From newspaper ads, cut pictures of three or four foods you'll be shopping for. Place them in an empty envelope and take them to the supermarket. Let your child pull out the pictures and remind you of what you need. If your child is holding a picture of apples, buy a few apples. If he is holding a picture of eggs, say, "Yes, we need eggs today."

**Quick Picture Puzzle**   Remove the front of your breakfast cereal box. Trim the edges and cut the picture into six or seven pieces. Your child will enjoy putting the pieces together. You can help her by pointing out ways to match part of a picture on one piece to another part of the picture on another piece. Good thinking!

**✻✻ Ages&Stages**

36–42 months

# *⁎⁎⁎ Personal-Social

## Activities to Help Your Child Grow and Learn

Your child is becoming more and more sociable. He can be very helpful with household tasks and can take care of many of his personal needs. He plays with other children but still may not be able to cooperate or share very well. Your approval and attention are very important to him. He likes being silly and making others laugh, especially you.

**Dress-Up Fun**  Let your child play dress-up in some old or interesting clothes. Boots are fun, as well as large hats. A scarf or necklace adds a nice touch. A purse, wallet, or vest also makes the play interesting. Make sure there are some buttons to button, some zippers to zip, or some gloves to stick fingers into for even more skill building! Put a mirror at your child's level. Ask her, "Are you ready to go to town?" "Are you going to work?"

**Counting Turns**  Help your child learn to manage taking turns by counting how long a turn will take. For example, tell your child he can swing until the count of 10, and then it will be his brother's turn. Count 10 swings out loud. "Okay, now it's your brother's turn for 10 swings. Help me count." Your child will learn that the wait for a turn will soon be over.

**Wonderful Rhythm and Rock**  In addition to stories, read poems and rhymes to your child at special cozy quiet times. If you have a rocking chair, cuddle up and rock a little to the rhythm of the words, or just cuddle and rock. Let your child fill in some of the missing words to a rhyme:

>        You:  Hickory, dickory...
> Your child:  dock
>        You:  The mouse ran up the...
> Your child:  clock

**Cupcakes for All**  Let your child help you bake some cupcakes for the family. Let her sift, pour, and stir as much as she is able. Let your child spread icing with a plastic knife while you do the cooking and handle anything hot. Talk about who the cupcake is for. Place it on a napkin and write that person's name on the napkin. At mealtime, let your child share the special cupcakes.

**Counting Good-Night Kisses**  When you put your child to bed, count kisses out loud. Ask your child how many kisses for the chin: "Three? Okay, one (kiss), two (kiss), three (kiss). How about your nose?" What a happy way to learn to count.

**Set the Table**  Let your child help you set the table. Place one plate on the table for each person, and then show your child how to put one fork by each plate, then one napkin by each fork. What a good helper!

*⁎⁎ Ages&Stages

## 36–42 months

# Communication

## Activities to Help Your Child Grow and Learn

Your child now enjoys longer books and stories. She can help tell a story or make up silly stories of her own. She probably asks "why" often, not only about books but also about daily events. She can describe recent events with some detail and with a little help can place the events in order. She may be reading familiar signs in the neighborhood and may know what words and letters are. She knows her first and last name and probably recognizes her name in print.

| | |
|---|---|
| **Talking Book** | Paste pictures that your child chooses, one per page, in an inexpensive notebook or on blank pages tied or stapled together. As you look through this picture book with your child, ask him to talk about the pictures. Say, "What's going on here?" "What colors do you see?" "Is that doggie happy or sad?" See if your child can tell you two or three things about each picture. |
| **Say What You Can See** | When you're on the bus or in the car, look for things in a certain category, alive or in pictures. Choose the category ahead of time. You might say, "Let's see how many animals we see while we're riding." Both you and your child can point out dogs and cats, as well as animals on posters, statues, and so forth. Try to find things with wheels or things that are tall. Let your child pick her own categories. |
| **My Own Stories** | Your child can begin to make up stories of her own. You can encourage her to tell the stories by writing them down on a piece of paper as she tells them to you. She might like to draw or paint a picture to go along with the story. You can put these stories in a folder to make a book titled "My Own Stories." |
| **Fill in the Blank** | When reading familiar stories, leave a word out here or there, and pause to let your child fill in the word or even the sound: "Mama Duck said, \_\_\_\_\_, \_\_\_\_\_, \_\_\_\_\_." |
| **Do What I Do** | Do a simple action, such as clapping your hands, and tell your child, "Do what I do." Then, add a second motion such as patting your stomach. Have your child do it with you first, then by himself. Now add a third motion and see if your child can remember all three: clap, clap, pat, pat, wink, wink. Add more as long as your child can remember them and as long as you both are having fun. |

Ages&Stages

42–48 months

# Gross Motor
## Activities to Help Your Child Grow and Learn

Your child is now more coordinated and will run, climb, swing, and balance with more confidence. He can jump, dance, and balance on one foot for longer than 1 second. He can walk heel to toe and begin to do forward somersaults. He may have the skills to pump on a swing.

**Follow the Leader**  When playing in the house, outside, or at the park, have your child follow you through an obstacle course. Activities might include over the cooler, around the blanket, hopping across the grass, walking backward, or sliding down a slide. When you finish, let her take a turn leading you through an obstacle course.

**Catch**  This is a good age to start to play catch with your child. Use a fairly big ball, preferably one that is soft so it won't hurt if he fails to catch it. Start by tossing the ball to him from a close distance, then move back so that he is practicing catching from 5 or 6 feet away.

**Freeze Game**  Play a little music, and move around with your child or several children. When you turn off the music, everyone is supposed to stop moving and "freeze" in a stiff position. Encourage your child to freeze in many different positions (e.g., on one foot, bent over, on tip toe). Say, "melt" and everyone can move again.

**Ring Toss**  Cut out the centers of plastic lids from coffee cans or other large cans to make large rings. Have your child toss the rings either onto a small post (made from a paper towel roll taped to a piece of cardboard) or a stick in the ground if you are playing outside. Your child might also aim for a box placed a few feet from her.

**Jumping**  When your child can jump and land with two feet at the same time, show him how to jump over something with height. Start with a book or blocks. See if your child can still keep two feet together.

**Toddler T-Ball**  Use an empty round ice cream carton, an oatmeal box, or any other round container as the stand for a medium-size ball or balloon. Let your child swing a small plastic bat or a cardboard roll from paper towels, aluminum foil, or gift wrap. This t-ball game is a lot of outdoor fun. Make up the rules. Have as many turns as your child wants. When your batter hits the ball, have her run into Daddy's arms!

Ages&Stages

42–48 months

# Fine Motor

## Activities to Help Your Child Grow and Learn

Your child has stronger finger muscles and is more skilled in drawing and writing. She can put puzzle pieces together and can string beads with ease. She's getting better at using scissors and may be able to cut on a line without help. She may even be able to trace over simple designs.

**Magazine Cutting and Pasting**
Give your child an old magazine and a pair of small safety scissors. Let him cut pictures out of the magazine (he doesn't have to cut them out perfectly) and, using a glue stick, glue them to a piece of paper. You can ask your child to choose a certain kind of picture. Tell him, "Find food that you like, and cut it out." "Cut out some coupons for Mommy."

**More Puzzle Pictures**
Take a colorful page from a magazine, cut it in five or six pieces, and encourage your child to put the pieces together. For sturdier puzzles, glue the pictures onto cardboard before you cut them. Save the puzzles in an envelope to use again and again.

**Where's the Button?**
Provide clothes for your child that have one or two large buttons. You might also let her help you fasten a button on something of yours. As she is trying to fasten the button, pretend it is a Hide-and-Seek game, with the button hidden at first, then "peeking out" from the hole, and then all the way through.

**Pick-Up Games**
Give your child a pair of tweezers or small tongs and two cups. Put some cotton balls, large pieces of macaroni, or large beans into one of the cups, and have your child pick them up with the tweezers and put them into the other cup. Once your child can do this, make it more exciting by having a race. Do it fast. Ready, set, go!

**Winding the Clock**
If you have a wind-up clock, show your child how to wind the alarm or turn the hands. Not only will your child get some good fine motor practice, but he also will learn something about how clocks work.

**Tool Time**
Let your child play with some large nuts and bolts. See if she can screw the nut onto the bolt. You might also let her try hammering a short nail into a piece of soft wood. If you have a fat screw with a large slit, let your child try her hand at using a simple screwdriver. You may need to hold on to the screw or make sure that the hole is large enough so that the task isn't too hard. Always supervise when kids are using tools.

Ages&Stages

42–48 months

# Problem Solving

## Activities to Help Your Child Grow and Learn

Your child is learning to count with some accuracy, up to three or four items. He can probably count up to 10 from memory. His knowledge about the world is growing. He now understands simple opposites and whether things are the same or different. He understands patterns, or degrees of change, such as "cool, warm, hot water" or "loud, louder, loudest."

**Remember What Happened When...** Encourage your child to tell you about things that happened in the past. You can start with this phrase: "Remember what happened when [you went to Grandma's and we went swimming]?" Follow up with questions such as "When did we do that?" "What did you like the best?" or "How did that make you feel?"

**Color Hunt** Have a scavenger hunt for colors. Say to your child, "Find something [color] and put it on the table." When she returns, give her another color. This is a fun game for everyone to play, including older children or adults. Try to use four or five different colors. Even if she brings back the wrong color, praise her for trying.

**Where Does the Sock Go?** Put a sock (of any type) on your head or somewhere else it doesn't belong. Ask, "Where is my sock?" When your child points or says it's on your head, ask him where it really belongs: "On my foot? Really?" Have fun with this silly game. Try another object, such as a bar of soap in a cereal bowl.

**What Do You Do When...** Ask your child simple questions such as "What do you do when you're really tired?" "What do you do when you get hungry?" "What do you do when you're all wet?" See if your child can give you answers that make sense. Talk about it.

**What Doesn't Belong?** Play this fun thinking game. Gather four things. Make sure three are very similar or are in the same category, such as three lemons. Add a fourth item that does not belong, such as a bar of soap. Ask your child to tell you which one doesn't belong. Try something different: Gather three things from the bathroom—such as soap, shampoo, or toilet paper—and add something such as a screwdriver. Ask your child to tell you what doesn't belong and why.

Ages & Stages

42–48 months

# Personal-Social
## Activities to Help Your Child Grow and Learn

Your child is better at taking turns and waiting. Although she plays with other children cooperatively, she still needs adult help from time to time with problem solving. Her feelings can be strong, but they may become easier to understand when you name them. She likes to select her own clothes and is more skilled at dressing herself.

**Pouring** Give your child a small pitcher or measuring cup and let him pour his milk from the pitcher into his cup or bowl of cereal. Have a paper towel ready just in case. Let him pour juice or milk at mealtime. Praise his success.

**Dress-Up** Provide clothes for your child to play dress-up. Children love to imitate adults in their family and in their community. The clothes don't have to be fancy, just oversized shirts, scarves, hats, skirts, shoes, or even loose fabric. Encourage children to dress themselves, fastening buttons, snaps, zippers, and so forth. Play along: "Are you going to work today?" "Are you going to a party?"

**Puppets** Puppets are another way to pretend and to have some fun. You can use store-bought puppets, or make them yourself. Find a magazine picture (or draw a picture) of a person or animal, cut it out, and paste it on cardboard. Attach a Popsicle stick, paint stirring stick, or chopstick for a handle. Let your child be one character, and you be another. Have conversations in pretend voices.

**Special Helper** Proclaim your child the special helper for the day. Let her help you wash the clothes, cook, feed pets, sweep, and wash dishes. She can help in some small way with almost everything. Be sure to allow extra time since young helpers may need it. This helping will eventually become part of your child's family chores, so be sure to give praise and keep it fun. At dinnertime, tell the others in the family what a great helper she was.

**Self-Help Choices** Offer choices to your child about his activities, including taking care of himself. Sometimes it is easier to get him to cooperate when he has a choice. For example, you might offer him the choice to brush his teeth either before or after he puts on his pajamas. These self-help skills are things children can start doing for themselves, but it's more fun and more appealing if there's a choice.

*✱✱✱*
Ages&Stages

42–48 months

# Communication
## Activities to Help Your Child Grow and Learn

Your child is learning new words every day, and he enjoys playing with language by rhyming words. He may use very silly language and laugh at his own jokes. He uses a lot of inflection (changes in his voice) when he describes events. He knows the difference between day and night, today and tomorrow. He can carry out three or more simple commands. He also knows that printed letters and words mean something to others.

**Puppets**
Puppets can be made in many different ways. You can use a small lunch bag, an old sock, or a paper circle glued on a Popsicle stick. Your child can make faces with crayons, markers, or paint. She can glue yarn or strips of paper for hair. Put on a puppet show of a familiar story or folktale. Have a conversation with the puppets, taking turns asking and answering questions.

**Adventure Pals**
Take your child on a special trip to someplace new. You could visit a museum, a park or outdoor area, a new store, or a library. Plan it with your child. Talk about what you will be seeing and doing. After you come home, ask him questions about what he saw and did. Encourage him to tell other family members about the outing.

**Feely Bag**
Gather some small objects from outside or around your house and put them in a paper bag. Let your child pick an item without looking, then have her try to guess what it is. If she has a hard time naming the item, help her along. For example, you could ask her, "Does it feel rough or smooth?"

**All About Me**
Have your child make a book about himself. Start by stapling or putting together several pieces of paper with tape or yarn or ribbon. Your child can glue pictures of family members or pictures of things he likes from magazines. He can trace his hand on a page or draw pictures. Have your child "read" you his story or tell you about each of the pictures.

**Big Helper**
Your child will enjoy helping you around the house. When it is mealtime, she could help set the table. Give her a few simple directions and see if she can remember the directions. For example, you could ask her, "Open the drawer, get four napkins, and put one on each plate." She may need some help remembering at first. Let her know what a big helper she is.

**Cloudy Friends**
This activity is fun on a day the sky is filled with puffy clouds. Lay on your back and take turns pointing out different cloud shapes and patterns. Ask your child what the clouds look like. "Does it look like an ice cream cone?" "That one looks like a dinosaur!"

Ages&Stages

48–54 months

# Gross Motor

## Activities to Help Your Child Grow and Learn

Your child is continuing to develop and refine her gross motor skills. She can ride a tricycle, weaving in and out of obstacles and stopping and turning with skill. She can kick a ball if you roll it into her path. She is learning to run and change direction without stopping and is learning how to somersault and gallop. She can keep herself going on a swing by pumping her legs back and forth and can throw a ball overhand about 10 feet.

**Air Balloon**    Play this game with your child and maybe one or two other friends. Keep a balloon in the air by tapping it once to send it up into the air. As it comes down, it's someone else's turn to tap it up once. See how long you can keep the balloon from falling to the ground.

**Target Practice**    Cut a few 8- to 9-inch holes out of a big piece of cardboard to make a target. Your child can decorate the target with paints. Prop the cardboard up, and let your child try to throw a tennis ball through the holes. Start by letting your child stand very close to the target, and then let him move back a few feet. Let him try throwing underhand and overhand. You can also pin a target on a tree or tape an X on a wall or fence.

**Ball Games**    Your child is ready to practice ball skills. Some games can be changed a little to make them easier. For example, a small trash can on a chair could be a hoop for a basketball. Use a big ball and show your child how to dribble and shoot to make a basket. Play soccer by using any two objects for goals and kicking the ball to get a goal.

**Scarf Dancing**    This is a great activity for a rainy day. Just turn on the radio, and your child can dance to the music. If you have scarves (or dishtowels), she can hold these in her hands while she dances. Try different kinds of music, such as rock and roll or whatever music your family enjoys. Encourage your child to listen and move to the rhythm.

**Circle Catch**    It's fun to play catch with your child and a few friends. Use a ball about the size of a beach ball or slightly smaller. Show the children how to hold out their arms to get ready for the ball. Stand in a circle and throw the ball to each other. Get ready. Now catch!

**Playground Time**    Bring your child to a neighborhood playground as often as possible. He will enjoy climbing, running, swinging, sliding, and learning new skills. Keep a close watch. He can be very daring!

Ages&Stages

48–54 months

# Fine Motor
## Activities to Help Your Child Grow and Learn

Your child's finger movements are more controlled now. For example, he can place small pegs in holes on a board and build a tower of small blocks (usually 9 or so). He is learning how to draw shapes following a model and may be learning how to write some letters. He can cut out circles and shapes with curved lines using safety scissors. With his controlled hand movements, he is able to do more tasks independently.

**Pudding Fun**  Make a batch of pudding in a bowl. Place a few spoonfuls on a cookie sheet or on a plate. (You may want to cover the table with newspaper first.) Have your child first wash her hands and then finger-paint in the pudding. Your child can draw pictures and practice drawing shapes or letters in the pudding. The best part is cleaning up! Yum!

**Book Making**  Books can be made from any type of paper. Just staple, tape, glue, or sew together a few pieces of paper. Then your child can make up his own book. On the pages, your child can draw pictures or paste in cut-out pictures from magazines to illustrate a story. Encourage him to tell you his story. Help him by writing down his words on each page.

**Signed by the Artist**  Have your child paint with watercolors at home or draw a picture with crayons. When your child finishes a picture, help her write her name. She may need your help at first. Then she can try to do it by herself. Encourage her in making the marks on the paper, even if they don't look just right. Doing activities by herself is how your child will learn.

**Paper Chains**  Paper chains can be made by cutting any type of paper into strips about 1 inch by 5 inches. Show your child how to make a loop by gluing or taping the ends together. Create a chain by inserting the next strip through the first loop and so forth. See how long you can make the chain.

**You've Got Mail**  When the mail comes to your home, let your child open the junk mail. He can exercise his fingers opening the mail, and he may find some little surprises inside. Help your child write and mail letters to family members or to a favorite performer or athlete.

**Water Painting**  On a dry, warm day give your child a plastic bucket of water, one or two paintbrushes, and an old sponge. Find a safe paved driveway, fence, or sidewalk and let him paint large pictures or patterns with the water on the cement or wood. Watch the pictures disappear.

Ages&Stages

48–54 months

# Problem Solving
## Activities to Help Your Child Grow and Learn

Your child's attention span is growing, and she can attend to an activity she enjoys without supervision. She is starting to sort according to shape, size, and length and can match items that look alike. She is also learning how things go together on the basis of function; for example, she can point to "all things that are tools" in a picture of multiple objects. Your child loves to read stories and is learning how to make up stories or story endings by herself. Wild stories and exaggerations are common.

**Rhyme Time**
When you are in the car or on a bus, play a rhyming game with your child. Think of a word, and have your child come up with a rhyme. Then, have your child think of a word and you find a rhyming word. For example, you say, "star," and your child says "car." Your child says, "train," and you say, "rain." If your child is having a hard time thinking of a rhyming word, help him out a little.

**Grouping and Sorting**
Gather together a lot of little things in a small container. You might already have a box in your home with buttons, coins, or odds and ends. Sit with your child and try to come up with ways to group the things together. For example, the two of you might sort buttons by color, size, or numbers of threading holes. Find the biggest button and the smallest button. Line up five items, and point to each one as you count. Now let your child try.

**Waiting Game**
When you and your child are waiting for something, try counting together to see how long it will take for the event to happen. For example, when you are in the car and waiting for the light to change to green, count how long it takes to change. She will learn how to count, and it may help her become more patient.

**Broadway Baby**
Read a story to your child, and then encourage him to act out the story. He can pretend to be different characters. For example, you might read a story about farm animals and he could pretend to be a cow, chicken, piggy, or horse. Encourage him to act out the beginning, the middle, and the end of the story.

**Number and Letter Search**
When you are at stores with your child, play number and letter searches. Encourage her to find numbers or letters on the walls, pictures, and signs. When she spots one, say, "You found the number 5. Good for you!" Point out numbers between o1ne and 9 or single letters of the alphabet. Ask your child to find something specific: "Now we're looking for the letter C."

Ages & Stages

48–54 months

# Personal-Social

## Activities to Help Your Child Grow and Learn

Your child is becoming more independent in dressing and has refined his skills. He can put his shoes on the correct feet. He uses the toilet without needing help and can brush his teeth. He is eating different types of foods and can serve himself at the table, pouring and scooping with no spilling. He plays cooperatively with other children and will comfort a playmate in distress. He plays games with rules and can follow directions.

**Game Time** — Your child may enjoy learning games that have rules. You can play card games with your child, such as Go Fish, Old Maid, or Animal Rummy or other games such as Candy Land or Don't Spill the Beans. If other children come over, you may need to play at first to help them learn about rules and taking turns.

**Super Chef** — Your child will love to help you cook or make her own snack. She can learn how to pour, stir, spread, and cut soft foods with your help (and careful supervision). You might try muffin pizzas. Your child can scoop spaghetti sauce on an English muffin, sprinkle on some cheese, and add toppings that she likes. Cook the muffin pizzas in the oven for a few minutes. Yum.

**Tent Safari** — On a rainy day, ask your child if he would like to invite a friend over to play. Give the children some old blankets or sheets and let them build a tent by draping the sheets over chairs or furniture. Once they make their tent, they can play in it or read books with a flashlight.

**Teddy Bear Picnic** — Your child can bring her stuffed animals or dolls on a picnic. Make a basket with a blanket, napkins, pretend food, and plastic plates and tea cups. Your child can practice dressing skills by getting "dressed up" for the bears. Later, your child can help clean up after a wonderful picnic.

**Novice Note Writer** — Help your child write a letter to someone he knows. Your child can draw a picture and you can write down the words he wants to say, or your child can try his own skills at writing. Show him how to address the envelope, and have him practice saying his full name and address. You can help your child write his name at the end of the letter.

**Rub-a-Dub** — Keep a sturdy footstool in the bathroom so that your child can step up and see herself in the mirror. Give your child her own special washcloth and towel, and teach her how to wash her face with soap. Give her a big kiss on her clean and shiny face! When she takes a bath, she can wash herself and dry herself off, too. Don't forget to have her brush her teeth.

Ages&Stages

48–54 months

# Communication

## Activities to Help Your Child Grow and Learn

Your child's communication skills are growing and blossoming. She is learning how to have conversations with people she knows and is starting conversations as well as responding to people's questions. She is learning different parts of speech and using more complicated sentences; for example, when describing something she might say, "It was a very big brown dog." She may use very silly language and laugh at her own jokes.

| | |
|---|---|
| **Animal Guessing** | This is a game the whole family can play. Cut out some pictures of animals from a magazine. Turn the pictures upside down and have one person at a time choose a picture. The other people playing ask yes/no questions to guess what the animal is (e.g., "Does the animal swim?" "Is it bigger than a cat?"). When someone guesses the animal correctly, it's another person's turn to choose an animal card and let the others guess. |
| **Bedtime Memories** | When it's time to go to sleep each night, have a soft talk with your child. Whisper to him, "What was your favorite thing that happened today?" Ask what else happened. Share your favorite event, too. |
| **Reading Adventures** | Read to your child every day. Read slowly and with interest. Use a finger to follow the words. Stop reading at times, and encourage your child to talk about the pictures and the story. Make this a special and fun time for you and your child. |
| **Moonbeams** | On a night when the moon is visible, find a place to lie down or sit outside with your child and look at the moon and stars. What do you see? Can you connect the stars to make a picture? Can you make out a face on the moon? Ponder what it would be like to be an astronaut flying into space in a rocket. What do you think it is like on the moon? What would you do there? How would you feel about being so far away from earth? |
| **Rhymes and Rhythm** | While chanting or singing a nursery rhyme, have your child tap it out on a drum, the bottom of a pot, or an oatmeal box. This musical activity can be made more challenging and interesting by adding new instruments such as bells, spoons, or shakers (small plastic containers filled with beans). Have some noisy fun with friends! |
| **At the Office** | Set up a little office for your child with notebooks, a toy phone, a computer keyboard, pencils and pens, a ruler, a calculator, and a calendar. Add some envelopes, paper, and stickers. Encourage her to pretend to go to work, write letters, type messages, and make notes for friends. Pretend with her; call her on the phone and ask her questions. |

Ages&Stages

54–60 months

# Gross Motor
## Activities to Help Your Child Grow and Learn

Your child is continuing to develop and refine his gross motor skills. He has become much more stable and is learning how to balance on one foot or walk along a narrow beam. He is learning skills such as jumping, hopping on one foot, and skipping. He will enjoy activities such as throwing, catching, and kicking balls. You will need to watch him closely as he may try some dangerous tricks. He can ride a small bike with training wheels.

**Fall Fun**  In the fall, take your child outside to play in the leaves. Rake the leaves into small piles. Chase each other around the piles, jump in them, or try to leap over them. Try burying each other in leaves or catching the leaves as they fall.

**Freeze Tag**  Get a group of children together with your child to play a game of Freeze Tag. Designate one person to be "it." The person who is "it" runs around trying to tag other children. If a child is tagged, she must "freeze" (not move). Another child who is not "it" may "melt" a frozen player by touching her. A "melted" player can run around again to avoid being tagged. Whoever is tagged and made "frozen" three times is the next "it."

**Splash Game**  This activity is good on a hot day. You, your child, and your child's friends can stand around a small plastic pool or bucket of water. Using a big ball (e.g., beach ball), take turns and try to make each other wet by throwing the ball hard at the water. Do not throw the ball at each other, just at the water. You can also just play catch. Of course, later you'll all want to get into the pool!

**Ribbon Dance**  Cut a piece of ribbon or a party streamer into 6-foot lengths. Your child can explore ways to make designs in the air. Try circles and loops, up and down movements, and figure eights. Now try all of these movements with two ribbons, one in each hand. Finally, move from place to place taking the ribbons with you. Put on some music to help make a "ribbon dance." Try skipping, running, and walking.

**Animal Games**  Cut pictures of animals out of a magazine. Turn them face down, and take turns choosing an animal with your child. You must act out the animal you drew, and your child has to guess what animal you are. Take turns so your child has to act out an animal for you to guess. If you draw a kangaroo, you must jump, jump, jump. If you draw a cheetah, you will probably need to run. If you draw a cat, you may relax and lick your paws or leap to catch a mouse. You may act out a giraffe by walking on tiptoes and stretching really tall.

*✻*✻
Ages&Stages

54–60 months

# Fine Motor

## Activities to Help Your Child Grow and Learn

Your child is now able to use her fingers in a more controlled way. Her finger movements are coordinated and faster, and she may be very interested in trying to write the letters of her name. Many children begin to prefer using one hand over the other during this time. Your child may be cutting out shapes with scissors and getting better at buttoning and tying her shoes.

**Lacing Cards**  Using safety scissors, your child can cut out simple pictures of familiar things from magazines and glue the pictures onto cardboard. With a paper punch, punch several holes around the outside of the picture. Tie a shoestring or heavy piece of yarn through one of the holes. Make sure the other end of the string has tape wrapped around it to make a firm tip. Your child can sew in and out around the edge of the card. For variation, have your child sew two cards together.

**Sidewalk Fun**  Decorate your sidewalks with beautiful chalk drawings. Colorful chalk can be found at any toy store and some supermarkets. Chalk is easy to wash off the sidewalk, or rain will wash it away. Don't forget to remind your child to sign his name!

**It's a Wrap**  Give your child a small sturdy box, some newspaper or wrapping paper, tape, and ribbon. Let her practice wrapping the box. Later she can wrap a real present for a friend in her very own way.

**Family Portrait**  Encourage your child to draw a picture of the family. When he is done, ask him to tell you about his picture. Your can write down what he says about his siblings, parents, pets, or grandparents and save his responses with the picture.

**Map It**  You and your child can make a map of your neighborhood. Go for a walk to start this activity, and point out streets, buildings, and nearby parks or other landmarks. Then, after the walk, use paper and pens or markers to encourage your child to make a map of what she remembers. You may need to help her get started with her map. If the neighborhood is too large, start by mapping your own house or her own room. Ask your child, "Where's your bed?" "How about your toy box?"

Ages & Stages

54–60 months

# Problem Solving
## Activities to Help Your Child Grow and Learn

Your child may be counting to 15 from memory and accurately counting 10 objects. He is able to follow directions when he is in a group activity and knows the rules at home and at school. He enjoys pretend play and may act out different roles with friends. Wild stories and exaggerations are common. He enjoys "reading" books and may have simple books memorized. He is really starting to understand how things work in the world and is endlessly curious about why things are the way they are.

**Pretzel Fun**
Make pretzel letters (or numbers). Pretzels can be made with pizza dough or pie crust dough. Cut the dough into strips and form numbers or letters out of the dough. Brush with a beaten egg, sprinkle with a little salt and bake until golden brown. Eat up an A, B, or C!

**Fun Food Coloring**
Most children love to experiment with food coloring. Let your child color her food. Here are some ideas: color scrambled eggs blue, color a glass of milk, add a drop of color to a piece of apple or to a slice of bread before toasting it, and color mashed potatoes. Ask your child to think of other ideas.

**How Long? How Many?**
Count how long your child can do a new skill, such as standing on one foot, or how many times he can bounce a ball. Celebrate each time he can do a new skill for a little more time. Let him count while you try something, such as balancing a book on your head. This will help your child practice new skills and counting.

**Storytime**
Tell a story to your child. Use different voices, body postures, and facial expressions to be different characters. Now it's your child's turn to tell a story. Encourage your little one to ham it up—and don't forget to be an appreciative audience.

**What's Missing?**
Lay out five or more different toys and give your child time to look at all of them. Now, hide a single toy at a time. See how long it takes your child to figure out which toy is missing. You may need to give her some clues at first. Once she guesses which toy is missing, hide a different toy. Now it's her turn to try to trick you!

**Find the Treasure**
This activity has to be planned well ahead of time. Hide "treasure" (e.g., a favorite snack, a small bag of old jewelry, a new toy) in a place your child is able to reach. Make drawings of all of the places you want your child to search (e.g., a TV, a mailbox) for the "treasure." Be sure to make the drawings simple and clear. Each clue should direct your child to a place where he will find the next clue until he eventually finds the "treasure."

Ages&Stages

54–60 months

# Personal-Social
## Activities to Help Your Child Grow and Learn

Your child is able to meet most of her personal needs but may need practice or help on some of the more difficult parts of a task, such as tying her shoes. She eats a variety of foods, has social dining skills, and is dressing herself. She enjoys playing with other children and working together on projects. She is beginning to use her words to help solve conflicts with friends.

**Going on a Date** Go on a "date" with your child. Go out to lunch, or go to see a movie. Before you go out, you and your child can get ready. He can put on a special shirt and pants, wash his hands and his face, use the potty, and brush his teeth. Show him a mirror so he can see how great he looks. Now go have fun! Be extra polite. Use "please" and "thank you" throughout your date.

**Fruit Salad** Make a fruit salad for lunch. You can use any favorite fruits such as grapes, bananas, apples, and oranges. Your child will enjoy washing, peeling, and scooping the fruit into a bowl. She could even help slice a soft fruit such as a banana with a butter or plastic knife. Add things to the salad that sound yummy such as yogurt or nuts. Your child can practice using a spoon and fork as she helps make and serve the fruit salad.

**Pressed Flower Cards** Collect flowers from your yard or neighborhood, a park, or a roadside. Flowers that are small and delicate work best because they press flat. Once you collect your flowers, place them between sheets of paper towels or newspaper and lay them between heavy books (such as old phone books). Then, give the flowers a few days to dry and flatten out. Glue these flowers on a piece of paper to make notecards for family and friends. Help your child write someone a special note.

**911** Talk to your child about what he should do if he gets lost or if there is an emergency in the house. Your child can learn how to dial 911 and give information to the operator. You can role-play this with your child using a pretend phone, but teach your child to use a real phone for a real emergency. Teach your child his name, address, and telephone number. Sometimes it helps if he learns this information as a song. Pretend you are a police officer, and your child can pretend, too.

**All by Myself** Make sure your child has a little extra time in the morning to get dressed. Then encourage her to try to button her shirt, snap her pants, or tie her shoes. She will need some help and some time, but be patient. The more she practices, the sooner she will be able to get dressed all by herself.

**You as Me, Me as You** You and your child can switch roles for part of the day. She can pretend to be you and help you get dressed or brush your hair. You can pretend you need help getting ready. The make-believe could include a change of duties, clothes, behaviors, vocabulary, and other habits. Keep the activity positive and fun.

✶✶✶ Ages&Stages

54–60 months

# Ages & Stages Questionnaires®

## A Parent-Completed, Child-Monitoring System, *Second Edition*

By Diane Bricker, Ph.D., & Jane Squires, Ph.D., with assistance from Linda Mounts, M.A.,
LaWanda Potter, M.S., Robert Nickel, M.D., Elizabeth Twombly, M.S., & Jane Farrell, M.S.

## The ASQ system includes:

**The Ages & Stages Questionnaires®—*English, Spanish, French, and Korean* versions:**\*

- 19 color-coded, reproducible questionnaires in English, Spanish, or French for use at 4, 6, 8, 10, 12, 14, 16, 18, 20, 22, 24, 27, 30, 33, 36, 42, 48, 54, and 60 months of age.
- 11 color-coded, reproducible questionnaires in Korean for use at 4, 6, 8, 12, 16, 18, 20, 24, 30, 36, and 48 months of age.
- Reproducible, age-appropriate scoring sheets—1 for each questionnaire
- 1 convenient storage box
- 1 reproducible mail-back sheet for questionnaires

**The ASQ User's Guide, *Second Edition* (in English):** This revised and expanded guide helps professionals accurately administer the questionnaires and confidently interpret their results.

**The Ages & Stages Questionnaires® on a Home Visit:** This 22-minute tutorial shows professionals how to conduct **ASQ** on home visits, with footage of a home visitor guiding a family with three children through the items on a questionnaire. Available on DVD or VHS.

**ASQ: Scoring & Referral:** This 16-minute tutorial shows how to score the questionnaires accurately and make informed decisions about referrals. Available on DVD or VHS.

**ASQ CD-ROM:** The PDF-format questionnaires, scoring sheets, and intervention activity sheets are available on CD-ROM in English or Spanish and can be printed or photocopied by a single site as needed. They can be posted on an internal office network for use by multiple people in one office (or by multiple people in multiple offices with the purchase a multi-site license).

**ASQ Manager:** This computer database program helps centers and agencies use **ASQ** more efficiently by storing records, scoring questionnaires, creating center-wide reports, and generating parent letters.

**Ages & Stages Learning Activities:** Fun, simple, and age-appropriate, these activities for children from 1 month to 5 years address the same five developmental areas as **ASQ.** Available in book or CD-ROM format.

**ASQ Materials Kit:** Ensure accurate, effective use of ASQ with this kit of approximately 20 sturdy, safe, easy-to-clean items. Comes with a tote bag and a booklet on how to use the kit with the questionnaires.

Don't miss the **Ages & Stages Questionnaires®: Social-Emotional!**
For more information, see ASQ:SE ad.

\*ASQ Questionnaires are available in other languages.

## TO ORDER

### call 1-800-638-3775 or visit www.agesandstages.com